D1521505

The Dalkey Archive Bibliography Series

I

THOMAS PYNCHON

Thomas Pynchon:
A Bibliography of Primary and Secondary Materials

Clifford Mead

The Dalkey Archive Press

WITHDRAWN
WESTERVILLE LIBRARY, NCC
NAPERVILLE, IL 60540

Copyright © 1989 Clifford Mead
All rights reserved

Library of Congress Cataloging in Publication Data
Mead, Clifford
  Thomas Pynchon: a bibliography of primary and secondary materials
  / Clifford Mead. — 1st ed.
    1. Pynchon, Thomas—Bibliography.   I. Title.
Z8721.5.M43   1989
[PS3566.Y55]
016.813'54—dc19   88-30415
ISBN: 0-916583-37-6

First Edition

Note: The texts by Thomas Pynchon quoted in section E and in the Appendix
are in the public domain.

Partially funded by grants from The National Endowment for the Arts and
The Illinois Arts Council.

The Dalkey Archive Press
1817 North 79th Avenue
Elmwood Park, IL 60635 USA

813.5
p99yme

Contents

Preface

Easter morning 1963, Thomas Pynchon, wearing a full-page advertisement in the *New York Times Book Review* for a first novel called *V.*, happened upon the spotlight of the world's literary stage. Soon after this arrival, he found a small fight taking place with erstwhile biographers and critics of his work on one side, his friends and family on the other.

Undoubtedly, he stood back a moment watching; then realizing he had one foot in the grave of celebrity anyway, Pynchon dived out of the way of the fight and lay more or less doggo, a position he has managed to maintain for the past quarter century.

Although this bout needs to go the distance before any final decision can be reached, it would certainly be useful for the spectators to sneak a look at the interim scorecard: Thus this book.

Thomas Pynchon: A Bibliography is organized into two parts. Part One is an enumerative bibliography of Pynchon's own work. The first section is a checklist of Pynchon's books, from *V.* in 1963 to *Slow Learner* in 1984. These entries begin with the first edition of each book and continue through all reprint editions. Although this bibliography does not consider proof copies to be true "editions"—they are little more than sophisticated photocopies—proofs and advance reading copies are included (when known) in a note following the first edition.

The next section cites all of Pynchon's separate contributions to books and periodicals, both fiction and nonfiction. It begins with a chronological listing of Pynchon's contributions to his high school newspaper, the Oyster Bay *Purple and Gold.* (While Pynchon prefers not to be judged by this early work, it is included here to complete the record.) Also included in this section are all anthologies containing works by Pynchon.

The third section lists piracies of Pynchon's work, and the fourth all known translations. The final section of Part One lists and reprints the published endorsements Pynchon has written for other books over the years.

Part Two is the bio-bibliography. Included are an alphabetical listing of books on Pynchon, books in which he or his work is significantly discussed, and periodical and newspaper material on Pynchon during the period from 1962 through 1988. While it attempts to be inclusive rather than selective, some trifles of negligible value have been omitted. Part Two concludes with a list of all known dissertations and theses on Pynchon's work, organized chronologically.

The appendix reprints trifles of a different sort—Pynchon's high school newspaper pieces. Although they are unsigned, these pieces are identified as Pynchon's in his high school yearbook, the *Oysterette*. Reproductions from this yearbook, which Pynchon himself edited, conclude the bibliography.

*

The first draft of this bibliography was compiled in 1980, a second draft was completed in 1982, and a revised and enlarged third draft was completed in 1985. Final revisions were made during 1988. During these various drafts, the work benefited from my correspondence with many people.

I am indebted to John Krafft and Khachig Tölölyan, the editors of *Pynchon Notes,* for sharing bibliographical tidbits on Pynchon with me over the years. *Pynchon Notes* remains the indispensable source for all current information on Pynchon scholarship.

I also gratefully acknowledge the help of the following people over the years: Mary Aiken, Cindy Ferguson, Kristin Johnson, Toby Levy, Edward Mendelson, Edith Nottman, Kristin Pintarich, Jagannath Raghu, Betsy Roberts, Richard Scaramelli, David Seed, and Mary Steckel.

A special debt of gratitude must go to Steven Moore, whose patience as an editor in developing the original typescript was exceeded only by his generosity as my friend.

—Clifford Mead

Part One

Primary Materials

A. BOOKS

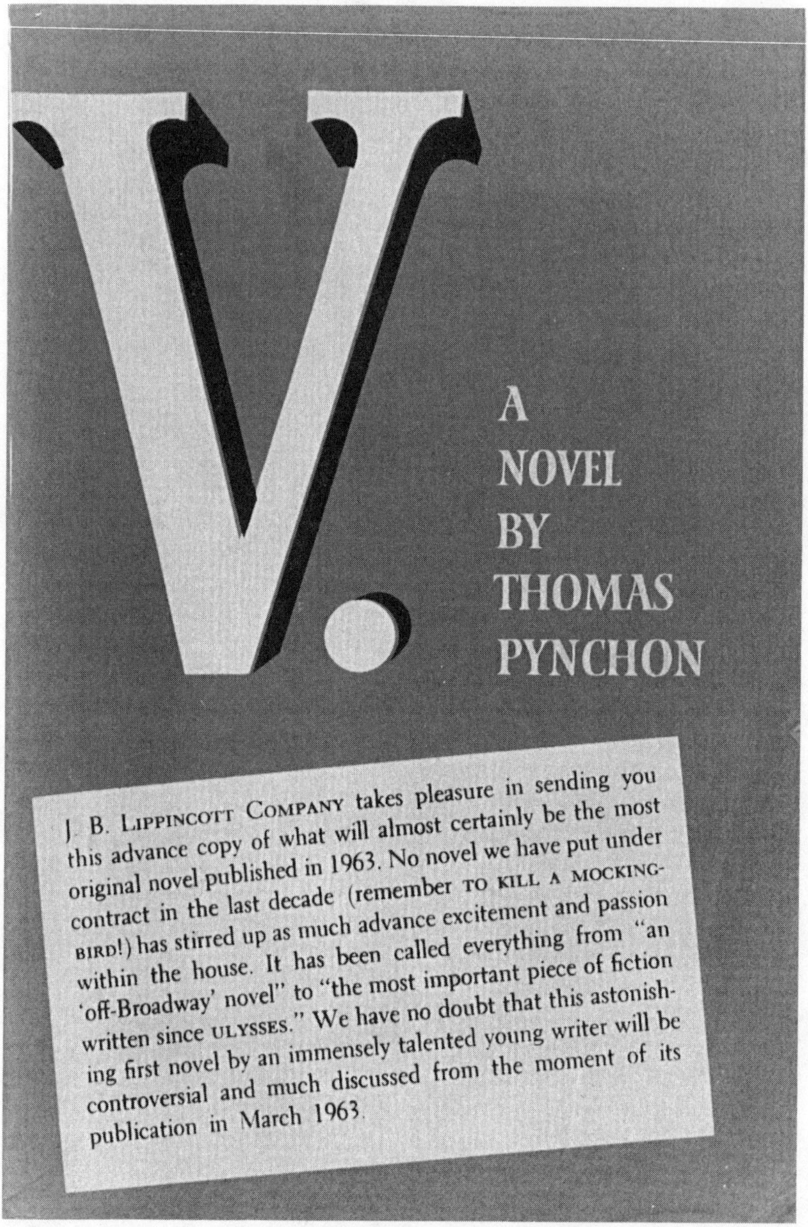
V.
A
NOVEL
BY
THOMAS
PYNCHON
J. B. LIPPINCOTT COMPANY takes pleasure in sending you this advance copy of what will almost certainly be the most original novel published in 1963. No novel we have put under contract in the last decade (remember TO KILL A MOCKINGBIRD!) has stirred up as much advance excitement and passion within the house. It has been called everything from "an 'off-Broadway' novel" to "the most important piece of fiction written since ULYSSES." We have no doubt that this astonishing first novel by an immensely talented young writer will be controversial and much discussed from the moment of its publication in March 1963.

A1a, *note*

A1a   Philadelphia: Lippincott, 1963. 492 pp. Second and third printings
       so stated.
           Note: this first edition was preceded by an advance reading copy
       in gray pictorial wrappers, with note from publisher on front cover.

A1b   London: Jonathan Cape, 1963. 492 pp. First British edition.
           Note: this edition was preceded by an advance proof copy in red
       wrappers.

A1c   New York: Bantam, 1964. 463 pp. First mass market paperback
       edition (Bantam Books N2748). At fourth printing becomes a
       "Bantam Modern Classic" (QY4203). At fifteenth printing
       becomes a "Bantam Windstone Book" (20332-0).

A1d   New York: Modern Library, 1966. 492 pp. First printing (so stated)
       in light green cloth, later printing(s) in dark green cloth.

A1e   Harmondsworth, Middlesex: Penguin, 1966. 485 pp. First British
       paperback edition.

A1f   London: Pan, 1975. 492 pp. First British trade paperback edition, a
       "Picador Book."

A1g   New York: Harper & Row, Perennial Fiction Library, 1986. 492
       pp. First American trade paperback edition.

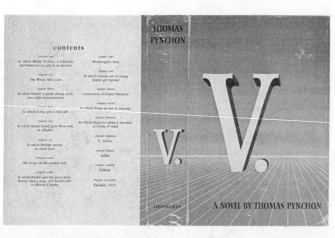

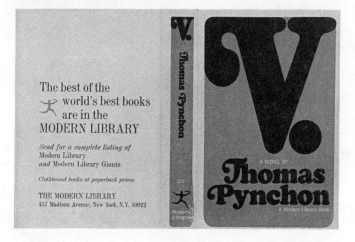

A1a, b, d

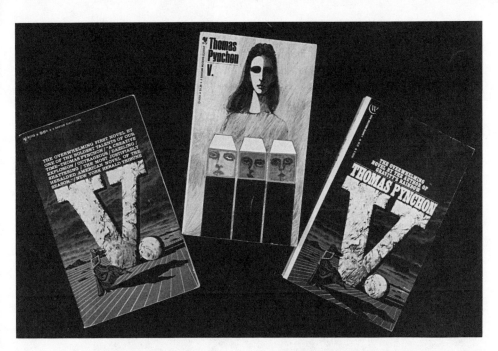

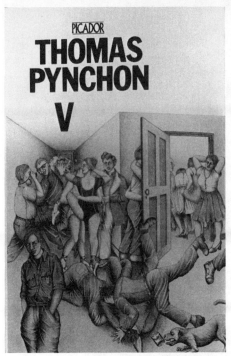

A1c (top), A1f (left), A1g (right)

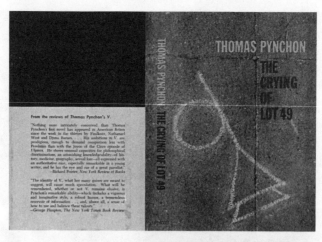

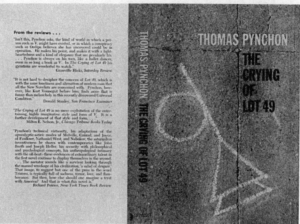

A2a (first and second printings), A2c

A2a   Philadelphia: Lippincott, 1966. 183 pp. Second printing so stated.
      Note: this first edition was preceded by an uncorrected proof
      copy in yellow wrappers in a plastic spiral binding.

A2b   London: Jonathan Cape, 1967. First British edition.

A2c   New York: Bantam, 1967. 138 pp. First mass market paperback
      edition (Bantam Books S-3384). At nineteenth printing becomes a
      "Bantam Windstone Book" (23691-1).

A2d   Harmondsworth, Middlesex: Penguin, 1974. 138 pp. First British
      paperback edition.

A2e   London: Pan, 1979. 127 pp. Second British trade paperback edi-
      tion, a "Picador Book."

A2f   New York: Harper & Row, Perennial Fiction Library, 1986. 183
      pp. First American trade paperback edition.

THOMAS PYNCHON

THE CRYING OF LOT 49

A NOVEL

"The comedy crackles, the puns pop, the satire explodes."—*New York Times*

BY THE AUTHOR OF *GRAVITY'S RAINBOW* AND *V.*

PL 1307/$4.95

A2f

Gravity's Rainbow, trial cover design

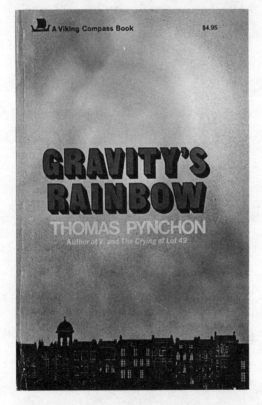

A3a   New York: Viking, 1973. 760 pp. Later printings so stated.
      Note: this first edition was preceded by two states of proofs:
      (1) pages sewn and glued into endpapers but not bound up, intended
      for major reviewers and readers for book clubs; (2) uncorrected
      proofs in blue wrappers.

A3b   New York: Viking, 1973. 760 pp. First trade paperback edition,
      issued simultaneous with cloth edition. Fourth printing contains
      corrections of some typographical errors.

A3c   New York: Viking, 1973. 760 pp. Book of the Month Club edition.
      Identical to A3a but on slightly thinner paper, no price or "0273"
      (month and year of publication) on jacket; contains code letters on p.
      [762], and a small blind-stamped square or maple leaf (no known
      priority) on lower right back cover.

A3d   New York: Viking, 1973. 760 pp. Quality Paperback Book Club
      edition. Identical to A3b but no price on front cover and code
      number "0365" printed on back cover.

A3e   London: Jonathan Cape, 1973. 760 pp. First British edition.

A3f   London: Jonathan Cape, 1973. 760 pp. First British paperback
      edition, issued simultaneous with cloth edition.

A3g   New York: Bantam, 1974. 887 pp. First mass market paperback
      edition.

A3h   London: Pan, 1975. 760 pp. Second British paperback edition, a
      "Picador Book."

A3i   New York: Penguin, 1987. 760 pp. Second American trade paper-
      back edition.

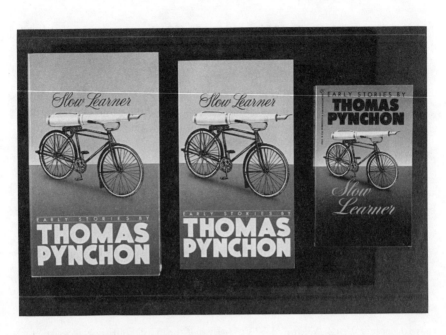

A4a, c, d (top), A4e (left)

A4a   Boston: Little, Brown, 1984. 193 pp. Contains an "Introduction" (3-23) and collects five stories: "The Small Rain" (B7), "Lowlands" (B9), "Entropy" (B10), "Under the Rose" (B12), and "The Secret Integration" (B13).

A4b   London: Jonathan Cape, 1985. 193 pp. First British edition.
     Note: this edition was preceded by an uncorrected proof copy in brick-red wrappers.

A4c   Boston: Little, Brown, 1985. 193 pp. First trade paperback edition.

A4d   New York: Bantam, 1985. 199 pp. First mass market paperback edition, a "Bantam Windstone Book."

A4e   London: Pan, 1985. 185 pp. First British paperback edition.

B. CONTRIBUTIONS TO BOOKS AND MAGAZINES

Purple and Gold

Published monthly by the students of
Oyster Bay High School

STAFF

Editor .... Tony Kohm
Advertising Manager .... Laura George
Advertising Assistants ...... June Henrich, Emily Koehler
News Editors ...... Ruth McConie, Mary Alice Fedoroff, Betty Meehan
Exchange Editor .... Mary Ann Piatt
Copy Editors .... Betty Ann Bruhns, Mary Thompson
Circulation Manager .... Robert Weitzman
Circulation Assistants ...... Gary Flower, Martin Olsen
Make-Up Editors ...... Herman Bowman, Peggy Disbrow, Joan Alfano
Sports Editors .... Charles Rothmann, Gladys Chisum
General Organization Editor .... June Crawford
Humor Editor .... John Nostrand

Proof Readers
Carla Hubbard, Althea Beglin
Special Writers
Denise Warren, Thomas Pynchon
Reporters
Dolores Srwejkowski, Virginia Furman, Dan Smolnik, Alyce Martin
Richard Zante, Bill Wylie, Carla Hubbard, Joan Parente
Typists
Virginia Tharp, Gladys Chisum, Lucille Iannicello
Joan Parente, Mary Alice Fedoroff

Managing Editor .... James George
Faculty Advisor .... Mr. Kasius

October 23, 1952 　　　　　　　　Fifteen Cents

EDITORIAL

RESPECT

Respect for your teacher is an important element in having a democratic form of school government. Lack of respect causes dictatorship to set in.

Many students seem to have forgotten the meaning of this word. I shall try to refresh your memory. It means to hold in high esteem and regard the rights of others. It does not mean a student may answer a teacher in a rude manner when being corrected or scolded for doing something wrong. Some hold a grudge for a failing mark on their report cards. Remember, if you get a failing grade it is through your own carelessness and stupidity.

Your mother's authority is turned over to your teacher as soon as you set foot in the school building. You treat your mother with respect; why not your teacher?

If we would all try to use more respect for both our teachers and fellow students the task of teaching and learning would be enlightened and more pleasant.

* * *

When the athletic awards are given out in Nassau County this year for outstanding football performance, Oyster Bay will not receive many of them. Few are given to the players on a losing team, but to the victor goes the glory. Many awards are given to high scoring halfbacks and important linemen. Still more are presented to flashing fullbacks and quarterbacks, but none are given for plain "guts."

Oyster Bay has, this year, shown that though they may be outclassed in weight, power, size, and experience they will go into a game and fight, fight, and then pick themselves up and fight some more. This team has refused to be beaten easily. Many boys, prior to this year, had never played in organized football before. Yet, when the time came, they went in and played against teams that had been playing together for years. Our players went into those games, stayed in and played their best. The best is all anyone can ask of a team, and that is what they gave.

We salute you, the members of the 1952 football squad.

* * *

Commendation must be given to Mr. Ruckel and his Teen-age Club for their fine work on the "Sock Hop." If the excellent turnout is any indication of how the students are and will be supporting the club, it should become one of the outstanding organizations of its type in this area. It would seem that this event may well have been the coming-out party of the Teen-age Club.

THE VOICE OF THE HAMSTER

Dear Sam,

You may remember me—I don't know. I met you at that party in Huntington last August. I was the squat individual with the red cravat who was doing the imitation of Winston Churchill. Anyway, you expressed interest in this school I go to and asked me to get in touch with you. So, here I am.

Hamster High is located on a rock about a half mile off the South Shore, and not a very big rock at that, as anybody can tell you who's been there at high tide. Nobody seems to know why they call the place Hamster High, other than the highly debatable rumor that its founder, J. Pattington Woodgrouse, had a strong liking for the faddy little creatures. There is a statue of J. Pattington Woodgrouse in front of the school. He is a little bald-headed man with a pot belly, and he looks like a cross between the last Martian and a hungry barracuda. Last Hallowe'en someone wrote on this statue a very nasty word in bright orange paint. There was a big scandal. I was suspended for four weeks.

Maybe the fact that we're fairly well isolated accounts for why Hamster High is—well, not exactly crazy, but—slightly odd. Take for example our trig teacher, Mr. Farginduiser. He's a quiet respectable young man who wears thick classes with chartreuse rims. He also wears peg pants, satin shirt, red cardigan, and dog beret. He tears around in a long, baby-blue hotrod sedan, and he's always telling be-bop jokes in class. There's nothing actually wrong with him, it's just that he used to be a bop drummer, and now he wishes he were back with the boys at Birdland and Eddie Condon's. He talks to himself a lot and I've heard rumors he takes heroin. A real "gone guy."

Then of course there's our principal, Mr. Sowfinkle. This boy also has music leanings—he plays the bagpipes. The bad thing about it is that he uses school hours to practice. He's very devoted to the bloody instrument. He locks himself in his office for about an hour every day to play it. Somehow one gets the idea he doesn't like interruptions. He was born in the hills of Tennessee, and he still carries a shot-gun with him, a nasty thing with a sawed-off barrel. Anyway, one day the chemistry teacher somehow wandered into his inner sanctum and started banging on the door, and old Park got real excited. Poor Miss Phipps. We had to get a new door, too.

You might think we're pretty limited as far as sports go, being out on a rock like we are, but that isn't so. Of course, we can't have our own football or baseball field, so we use the ones in the nearest town, Riverhampton. I feel sorry for Coach Willis. He turned down a chance to coach Football at one of the Big Ten colleges and came to Hamster High instead. Coach Willis drinks a lot.

He smokes like a fiend, too, so that the Annual Association is screaming bloody murder at the Administration to fire him for setting a bad example for the boys.

Coach Willis claims that it's the teams that have driven him to drink. He says: "What can you do with a football team that consistently runs the wrong way, a basketball team which refuses to dribble the ball, and a track team which is afraid to high jump, and throws the shot-put underhand?" In a way, I think he's right, about football, at least. In the past three years we've lost every game we've played except one, and that was a tie with some grade school. The only reason we were able to tie them was because the grade school team was continually being penalized for unnecessary roughness.

But still the crowds come out and cheer for our boys, so colorful and manly-looking in their brown fur football uniforms, and they cheer our loyal little team mascot, keep Talleyrand mantled and on a long leash, for he is a vicious little monster. This hamster has razorsharp fangs which must be at least an inch long. If you don't believe me, I can show you the scars where Talleyrand autographed my wrist.

But now I must say so long because I am getting tired, and I have a lot of trig homework to do. Not that it has to be done for tomorrow, as chances are Mr. Farginduiser won't be there; he's out on another binge. Remind me sometime to tell you about the time the State Education Inspector came to Hamster High. Poor fellow—he's in an institution, now. And remember me to Somebody Mac Pherson and the rest of the mob.

Your drunken buddy,
Bosco Stein

P & G MOVIE REVIEW

*—Indicates films recommended by P-G staff critics.
**—Indicates films that are fair.
***—Indicates stay at home.

"WITHOUT A MATCH"—Highly interesting Melodrama of a professional cigarette teacher, who falls in love with a torch singer. A warm human drama, but mild in spots.

"SIX GUNS, WEST OF THE ROCKIES"—Howard Butter Slick does an excellent job of portraying the dean of a small New England college. Also Marlene Comalitiklower.

"RED MEAT"—Heart-warming story of a man-eating tiger named Augustus, who is loose in Times Square on New Year's Eve.

"THE U. S. GOVERNMENT"—A rollicking cowboy, war in Washington, starring some of the biggest actors in the nation.

"48 OR BUST"—An exciting story of a schoolboy in June. The highpoint of the picture includes some hotrod sequences.

"TRICK OR TREAT"—The moving story of Old Uncle Wes, a candy manufacturer. A loveable old man who poisons children's jelly beans.

Also Playing
"LAMENT OF THE LOCUST."
"LOW MIDNIGHT."
"WHEN THE MOON COMES OVER THE HILL, THE STILL MUST CLOSE."

Our faculty spotlight this month focuses on Mr. Morris Chefee, our new Driving Education instructor. He also teaches science and health.

Mr. Chefee is 5' 10", weighs 155 lbs. and was born on December 27, 1927 in New York City. He attended Seward Park High School, where he was very active in basketball, having been on the varsity team for 4 years (he didn't take a P.G., either?).

After graduation from high school, Mr. Chefee furthered his studies as a student at C.C.N.Y. However, Uncle Sam's call interrupted his education; he was drafted into the Air Corps in 1945. He worked in the clerical department at Eglin Field, Fla., and was later stationed in Mississippi and Colorado. After being discharged, Mr. Chefee returned to complete his studies for his B.S. degree at, you guessed it, C.C.N.Y.

While there, he played 3 years of varsity basketball and 1 year of a crosse, which accounts for his majoring in physical education. He was elected vice-president of the Physical Education Society at C.C.N.Y. in 1949.

Mr. Chefee's wide variety of activities was displayed by his participation as recreation supervisor at the Jasper Oval, where he organized outdoor work for different race groups. This he did for two years as part of a sociological project. He was also recreation teacher at P.S. 50 in Manhattan for a year and a half.

Having been graduated in 1950, Mr. Chefee was appointed Recreation Director in Goversville, N. Y., for two years. Here he helped to organize social educational athletic activities for children of all ages. He also directed a summer day camp comprised of 75 youngsters whose varsity basketball team he coached to the championship of the Upstate Youth League.

When questioned about his family life, Mr. Chefee readily replied that he and his wife, whom he married in 1950, are living in Bayside but plan to move to the Garden Apartments in Little Neck when this project is completed. Mrs. Chefee attended L.I.U. and is now attending C.C.N.Y., where she is studying for her B.S. degree in education. Mr. Chefee, not forgetting his earlier years in college, is now doing graduate work at C.C.N.Y., where he is majoring in guidance.

By this time, you must think that Mr. Chefee has time for nothing else, but again he fools us, for he has many hobbies. These include collecting folk songs and classical records, square dancing, basketball and, above all, camping.

In 1949, Mr. Chefee was a member of the C.C.N.Y. basketball team which played in Madison Square Garden in the National Invitation Tournament. He scored 1 point, of which he is very proud.

B1 (date on masthead incorrect)

18

B1   "Voice of the Hamster." *Purple and Gold* 9, no. 2 (13 November 1952): 2.

B2   "Voice of the Hamster." *Purple and Gold* 9, no. 3 (18 December 1952): 3.

B3   "Voice of the Hamster." *Purple and Gold* 9, no. 4 (22 January 1953): 2, 4.

B4   "Voice of the Hamster." *Purple and Gold* 9, no. 5 (19 February 1953): 8.

B5   "Ye Legend of Sir Stupid and the Purple Knight." *Purple and Gold* 9, no. 6 (19 March 1953): 2.

B6   "The Boys." *Purple and Gold* 9, no. 6 (19 March 1953): 8.

B7   "The Small Rain." *Cornell Writer* 6, no. 2 (March 1959): 14-32. Collected in *Slow Learner* (A4).

B8a   "Mortality and Mercy in Vienna." *Epoch* 9, no. 4 (Spring 1959): 195-213.

B8b   ———. In *Stories from "Epoch": The First Fifty Issues (1947-1964),* edited by Baxter Hathaway. Ithaca: Cornell University Press, 1966. 181-201.

B9a   "Low-lands." *New World Writing 16.* Philadelphia: Lippincott, 1960. 85-108. Cloth edition. Collected in *Slow Learner* (A4).

B9b   ———. *New World Writing 16.* Philadelphia: Lippincott, 1960. 85-108. Paperback edition, issued simultaneous with cloth edition.

B9c   ———. In *The World of Modern Fiction: American,* edited by Steven Marcus. New York: Simon & Schuster, 1966. 496-511.

B9d   ———. In *American Literature,* edited by Richard Poirier and William L. Vance. 2 vols. Boston: Little, Brown, 1970. 2:1140-52.

B9e   ———. In *Modern Satiric Stories: The Impropriety Principle,* edited by Gregory FitzGerald. Glenview, Ill.: Scott, Foresman, 1971. 224-44.

spring 1959

35 cents   CORNELL WRITER

THE CORNELL WRITER

Volume VI, Number 2   March, 1959

• • • • • •

Donald R. Moyer, *editor-in-chief*

Stephanie Greene, *managing editor*

Trudy Cahane, *prose editor*   Margot Hebberd, *poetry editor*

Harriet Benjamin, Sue Overby, *art editors*

Dave Drucker, *business manager*

Editorial Board: Tom Pynchon, Roger Fogelman, Florence Cassen, Lillian Laufgraben, Larry Lesser, Julie Werner, Linda Eisen, Burt Sabol.

Junior Board: Leah Benin, David Nalin, Marcia Stone, Ed Ochester, Ellen Werman, Judy Bookstaber, Richard Klein, Grace Ganz, Tom Goldman.

Art Board: Sid Tamm, Georgia Bennett

Faculty Advisers: James McConkey, Baxter Hathaway

Published three times yearly by students at Cornell University.

The Editors of the CORNELL WRITER wish to express their appreciation to readers, advertisers and contributors whose interest and support have made this fifth year of publication possible. Material may be submitted throughout the year at Willard Straight main desk under the name of the WRITER.

B7

B10a   "Entropy." *Kenyon Review* 22, no. 2 (Spring 1960): 277-92. Collected in *Slow Learner* (A4).

B10b   ———. In *The Best American Short Stories: 1961*, edited by Martha Foley and David Burnett. Boston: Houghton Mifflin, 1961. 300-313.

B10c   ———. In *The Best American Short Stories: 1961*, edited by Martha Foley and David Burnett. New York: Ballantine, 1961.

B10d   ———. In *Nelson Algren's Own Book of Lonesome Monsters*. New York: Lancer, 1962. 157-72. This paperback edition precedes the cloth edition.

B10e   ———. In *Nelson Algren's Own Book of Lonesome Monsters*. New York: Bernard Geis, 1963. 177-91.

B10f   ———. In *Gallery of Modern Fiction: Stories from the "Kenyon Review,"* edited by Robie Macauley. New York: Salem Press, 1966. 51-65.

B10g   ———. In *Twelve from the Sixties,* edited by Richard Kostelanetz. New York: Dell, 1967. 22-35.

B10h   ———. In *New Worlds* [London] 187 (February 1969): 50-56.

B10i   ———. In *Modern Short Stories: The Uses of Imagination,* edited by Arthur Mizener. 3rd ed. New York: Norton, 1971. 430-44.

B10j   ———. In *Introduction to Fiction,* compiled by Paul J. Dolan and Joseph T. Bennett. New York: John Wiley, 1974. 195-206.

B10k   ———. In *The American Tradition in Literature,* edited by George Perkins et al. 6th ed. 2 vols. New York: Random House, 1985. 2:1909-13.

B10l   ———. In *The Harper American Literature,* edited by Donald McQuade et al. 2 vols. New York: Harper & Row, 1987. 2:2219-28.

B10m   ———. In *Contemporary American Literature,* edited by George Perkins and Barbara Perkins. New York: Random House, 1988. 589-98.

AEROSPACE
SAFETY
UNITED STATES AIR FORCE

THE MISSILES   DECEMBER 1960

T-33 PILOTS
Check Pages 26-27-28

"TOGETHERNESS"

Thomas H. Pynchon, Bomarc Aero-Space Dept., Boeing Airplane Co., Seattle

Airlifting the IM-99A missile, like airlifting anything, demands a certain amount of "togetherness" between Air Force and contractor. Two birds per airlift are unloaded by Boeing people and offloaded by Air Force people; in between is an airborne MATS C-124. One loading operation is a mirror image of the other, and similar accidents can happen at both places. Let's look at a few of the safety hazards that have to be taken into account when these are shipped.

One mistake and a lot of money has been wasted when you're moving a missile to its new home. It's a job requiring detailed safety on all sides. Togetherness, then, is the word.

AEROSPACE SAFETY

B11   "Togetherness." *Aerospace Safety* 16, no. 12 (December 1960): 6-8.

B12a   "Under the Rose." *Noble Savage* 3 (1961): 233-51. Collected in *Slow Learner* (A4).

B12b   ———. In *Prize Stories 1962: The O. Henry Awards,* edited by Richard Poirier. Garden City: Doubleday, 1962. 49-78.

B12c   ———. In *Prize Stories 1962: The O. Henry Awards,* edited by Richard Poirier. Greenwich, Conn.: Fawcett, 1963. 49-78.

B12d   ———. In *American Short Stories Since 1945,* compiled by John Hollander. New York: Harper & Row, Perennial Classics, 1968. 392-424.

B12e   ———. In *Fifty Years of the American Short Story: From the O. Henry Awards 1919-1970,* edited by William Abrahams. New York: Doubleday, 1970. 160-85.

B13a   "The Secret Integration." *Saturday Evening Post* 235 (19-26 December 1964): 36-37, 39, 42-44, 46-49, 51. Collected in *Slow Learner* (A4).

B13b   ———. In *Best Modern Short Stories Selected from the "Saturday Evening Post."* New York: Curtis Books, 1965. 448-85.

B14a   "In Which Esther Gets a Nose Job." In *Black Humor,* edited by Bruce Jay Friedman. New York: Bantam, 1965. 1-16. From *V.*

B14b   ———. In *SuperFiction, or the American Story Transformed,* edited by Joe David Bellamy. New York: Vintage, 1975. 137-53.

B15a   Letter, quoted by Jules Siegel, "The Dark Triumvirate." *Cavalier* 16, no. 146 (August 1965): 16.

B15b   Letter reprinted in Steven Moore, " 'The World Is at Fault.' " *Pynchon Notes* 15 (Fall 1984): 84-85.

B16   "A Gift of Books." *Holiday* 38, no. 6 (December 1965): 164-65.

B17   "The World (This One), the Flesh (Mrs. Oedipa Maas), and the Testament of Pierce Inverarity." *Esquire* 64 (December 1965): 170-73, 196. From *The Crying of Lot 49.*

B17 and B18

24

B18   "The Shrink Flips." *Cavalier* 16, no. 153 (March 1966): 32-33, 88-92. From *The Crying of Lot 49*.

B19a   "A Journey into the Mind of Watts." *New York Times Magazine*, 12 June 1966, 34-35, 78, 80-82, 84.

B19b   ———. In *Man against Poverty: World War III*, edited by Arthur Blaustein and Roger Woock. New York: Random House, 1968. 146-58.

B19c   ———. In *The California Dream*, edited by Dennis Hale and Jonathan Eisen. New York: Macmillan, 1968. 251-61.

B19d   ———. In *The California Dream*, edited by Dennis Hale and Jonathan Eisen. New York: Collier Books, 1968. 251-61.

B19e   ———. In *American Society Since 1945*, edited by William L. O'Neill. Chicago: Quadrangle Books, 1969. 217-28.

B19f   ———. In *Unknown California*, edited by Jonathan Eisen and David Fine. New York: Macmillan, 1985. 294-303.

B19g   ———. In *Unknown California*, edited by Jonathan Eisen and David Fine. New York: Collier Books, 1985. 294-303.

B20   "Pros and Cohns." Letter to the editor. *New York Times Book Review*, 17 July 1966, 22, 24.

B21   "From *The Crying of Lot 49*." In *The World of Black Humor: An Introductory Anthology of Selections and Criticism*, edited by Douglas M. Davis. New York: Dutton, 1967. 214-28. A paperback original. Reprints chap. 2.

B22   "V. in Love." In *The Single Voice: An Anthology of Contemporary Fiction*, edited by Jerome Charyn. New York: Collier Books, 1969. 137-58. A paperback original. From *V*.

B23   Letter to Richard Wilbur, in "Presentation to Thomas Pynchon of the Howells Medal for Fiction of the Academy." *Proceedings of the American Academy of Arts and Letters and the National Institute of Arts and Letters* 26 (second series) (1976): 43-46.

B24   Letter to the editor, quoted by John Calvin Batchelor, "The Ghost of Richard Fariña." *Soho Weekly News* 4, no. 30 (28 April-4 May

The New York Times Magazine

CAUTIOUS CRUSADER—The man who has made the nation auto-safety-conscious, Senator Ribicoff, poses beside a highway in Washington. [See Page 32]

JUNE 12, 1966 · SECTION 6 / Contents—Page 22

B19a

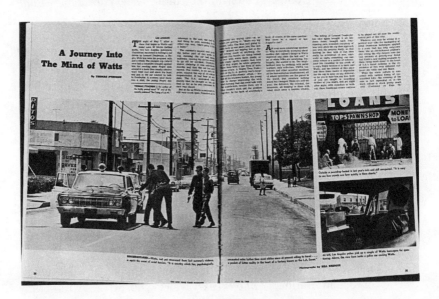

A Journey Into The Mind of Watts

By THOMAS PYNCHON

THOMAS PYNCHON is the author of the highly praised novel "V" and of the recently published "The Crying of Lot 49."

Photographs by BILL BRIDGES

26

1977): 20.

B25   "[From] *Gravity's Rainbow.*" In *America in Literature,* edited by
Alan Trachtenberg and Benjamin DeMott. 2 vols. New York:
John Wiley, 1978. 2:1455-62.

B26   "*The Crying of Lot 49.*" In *Forms of the Novella: Ten Short
Novels,* edited by David H. Richter. New York: Knopf, 1981. 718-
833.

B27a "Introduction." In Richard Fariña, *Been Down So Long It Looks
Like Up to Me.* New York: Viking, 1983. v-xiv.

B27b ———. Richard Fariña, *Been Down So Long It Looks Like Up to
Me.* New York: Penguin, 1983. v-xiv. Paperback edition, issued
simultaneous with cloth edition.

B27c "Pynchon Remembers Fariña." *Cornell Alumni News* 86, no. 10
(June 1984): 20-23. Reprint of B27a.

B28   "Is It O.K. to Be a Luddite?" *New York Times Book Review,* 28
October 1984, 1, 40-41.

B29   "From *The Crying of Lot 49.*" In *The Norton Anthology of
American Literature,* edited by Nina Baym et al. 2nd ed. 2 vols.
New York: Norton, 1985. 2:2217-37. Reprints chaps. 1 and 2
from the novel.

B30   "The Heart's Eternal Vow." Review of García Márquez's *Love
in the Time of Cholera. New York Times Book Review,* 10 April
1988, 1, 47, 49.

B31   Letter to Thomas F. Hirsch, quoted by David Seed, *The Fictional
Labyrinths of Thomas Pynchon.* London: Macmillan, 1988; Iowa
City: University of Iowa Press, 1988. 240-43.

B27a (overleaf)

27

It Looks Like Up to Me

THE CLASSIC NOVEL OF THE 1960s

Richard Fariña

Been Down So Long

NEW INTRODUCTION BY
THOMAS PYNCHON

C. UNAUTHORIZED EDITIONS

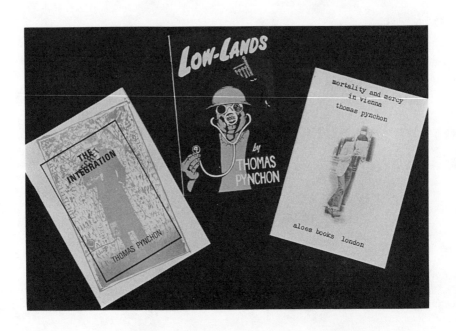

Cla   *Mortality and Mercy in Vienna.* London: Aloes Books, [1976].
Unnumbered (22 pp.). Smooth wrappers.

In a letter dated 4 February 1977 to Edward Mendelson, collector Gary M. Lepper described four different issues of this title, of no known priority, which he described as follows:

(1) Cover color is only red; neither the cross above the letter "p" nor the cross to the right of the man's hips shows any trace of a second color: both crosses are red.

(2) Cover color is brownish with the cross above the "p" being a larger green cross almost congruently laid over a smaller red cross; most importantly, the cross to the right of man's hip is missing.

(3) Cover color slightly more reddish, but basically the same color as (2); both crosses are present as in (1), but they are double crosses as in (2). The green cross is higher than the red cross and the intersection of the green lines is to the right of the intersection of the red lines.

(4) As (3), but the vertical lines of both crosses are congruent and the intersection of the green lines is to the left of the intersection of the red lines.

Clb   ———. London: Aloes Books, 1976. Second printing, in rough wrappers.

C2   *Low-Lands.* London: Aloes Books, 1978. Unnumbered (24 pp.). Wrappers. 1500 stated print run.

C3   *The Secret Integration.* London: Aloes, 1980. 47 pp. Wrappers. 2500 copies stated print run.

C4a   *Entropy.* Troy Town [England]): Tristero, 1957 [*sic*—actually 1981). 16 pp. Green wrappers with black stamping.

C4b   ———. Troy Town [etc., as above], actually 1983. Second printing. White wrappers with photograph montage on front and back covers.

C5   *The Small Rain.* London: Aloes Books, [1982]. Unnumbered (14 pp.). Wrappers.

C6   *A Journey into the Mind of Watts.* Westminister, England: Mouldwarp, 1983. 12 pp. Wrappers. With a "Justification" by "Tristero" (p. 12).

D. TRANSLATIONS

1. *V.*

D1a   *V.* Italian translation by Liana M. Johnson. Milan: Rizzoli Editore, 1965. 551 pp.

D1b   *V.* French translation by Minnie Danzas. Paris: Plon, 1967. 485 pp.

D1c   *V.* German translation by Dietrich Stössel. Dusseldorf: Rauch, 1968. 525 pp.

D1d   "Ona wisi na zachodniej scianie" [chap. 7 of *V.* after the introductory section]. Polish translation by Jacek Laskowski. *Literatura na Świecie* 6, no. 16 (1976): 4-93.

D1e   *V.* German translation by Dietrich Stössel and Wulf Teichmann. Epilogue by Elfriede Jelinek. Reinbek bei Hamburg, West Germany: Rowohlt-Taschenbuch, 1976. 551 pp.

D1f   "Wanigari" ["Alligator Hunt" from chap. 5 of *V.*]. Japanese translation by Masao Shimura. *Umi* 10, no. 6 (June 1978): 221-30.

D1g   *V.* Japanese translation by Takuo Miyake, Sadamoto Ito, Yukiko Nakagawa, Eiichi Hirose, and Koichi Nakamura. Tokyo: Tosho Kanko Kai, 1979. 2 vols.

D1h   *V.* Korean translation by Kim Sang-kun. Seoul: Hakwon-sa, 1983. 2 vols. (315 + 271 pp.).

D1i   *V.* French translation by Minnie Danzas. Paris: Seuil, 1985. 542 pp.

2. The Crying of Lot 49

D2a   *Buden på nr 49.* Swedish translation by Caj Lundgren. Stockholm: Wahlström & Widstrand, 1967. 172 pp.

D2b   *L'Incanto del lotto 49.* Italian translation by Liana M. Johnson. Milan: Rizzoli Editore, 1968. 206 pp.

D2c   *Katalognummer 49 udbydes.* Danish translation by Arne Herløv Petersen. Copenhagen: Glydendals Bekkasinbøger, 1968. 164 pp.

D2d   *Die Versteigerung von No. 49.* German translation by Wulf Teichmann. Reinbek bei Hamburg, West Germany: Rowohlt-Taschenbuch, 1973. 155 pp. Wrappers.

D2e   *San Francisco cry.* French translation by Michel Doury. Paris: Plon, 1976. 192 pp.

D2f   *La Subasta del lote 49.* Spanish translation by Veronica Head. Madrid: Editorial Fundamentos, 1976. 208 pp.

D2g   *Katalognr 49.* Norwegian translation by Olav Angell. Oslo: Gyldendal, 1977. 173 pp.

D2h   *De Veiling van nr 49.* Dutch translation by Ronald Jonkers. Amsterdam, 1978. 131 pp.

D2i   "Kyobaihin 49-ban no sakebi" [chaps. 1-3 of *Lot 49*]. Japanese translation by Masao Shimura. *Umi* 10, no. 6 (June 1978): 231-71.

D2j   *"49 idzie pod młotek"* [complete novel]. Polish translation by Piotr Siemion. *Literatura na Świecie* 7/168 (1985): 3-196.

D2k   *Kyôbai nambâ 49 no sakebi.* Japanese translation by Masao Shimura. Tokyo: Sanrio, 1985.

D2l   *Vente à la criée du lot 49.* French translation by Michel Doury. Paris: Seuil, 1986. 216 pp.

3. *Gravity's Rainbow*

D3a   *Rainbow.* French translation by Michel Doury. Paris: Plon, 1975. 663 pp. Pictorial wrappers, orange wraparound band.

D3b   *El Arco iris de gravedad.* Spanish translation by Antoni Pigrau. Barcelona: Ediciones Grijalbo, 1978. 2 vols. (595 + 515 pp.).

D3c   "Juryoku no niji" [excerpts from *Gravity's Rainbow*]. Japanese translation by Masao Shimura. *Umi* 10, no. 6 (June 1978): 272-313.

D3d   *Die Enden der Parabel.* German translation by Thomas Piltz and

Elfriede Jelinek. Reinbek bei Hamburg: Rowohlt, 1981. 1193 pp.

D3e "Tęcza grawitacji (fragmenty)" [from part 1 of *Gravity's Rainbow*]. Polish translation by Piotr Siemion. *Literatura na Świecie* 7/168 (1985): 225-45.

D3f *L'Arc-en-ciel de la gravité.* French translation by Michel Doury. Paris: Seuil, 1988. 761 pp.

4. Slow Learner

D4a *L'Homme qui apprenait lentement.* French translation by Michel Doury. Paris: Seuil, 1985. 194 pp.

D4b *Spätzunder: Frühe Erzählungen.* German translation by Thomas Piltz and Jürg Laederach. Reinbek: Rowohlt Verlag, 1985.

5. Short stories

D5a "Entropi" [Entropy]. Japanese translation by Kenji Inoue. In *Gendai amerika tampen senshu.* Tokyo: Hakusui-sha, 1970. 3:195-215.

D5b ———. Reprinted in *Gendai amerika genso shosetsu* [Contemporary American Fantastic Stories], edited by Masao Shimura. Tokyo: Hakusui-sha, 1973. 141-58.

D6a "Entròpia" [Entropy]. Hungarian translation by Istvàn Bart. In *Chicago ostroma,* edited by Mihàly Sukosd. Olcso Konyvtar, Hungary: K. Szépirod, 1977. 140-58.

D6b ———. Reprinted in *Entròpia: Mai amerikai elbeszèlok,* edited by Istvàn Bart. Modern Konyvtar, Hungary: Euròpa, 1981. 5-24.

D7 "Himitsu no integration" [The Secret Integration]. Japanese translation by Masao Shimura. *Umi* 12, no. 5 (May 1980): 292-328.

D8   *Pynchon's Short Stories,* edited by Masao Shimura. Tokyo: Nan'un-do, n.d. Contains "Low-lands" and "The Secret Integration" in English, introduction and notes in Japanese.

D9   "Ha-Mavet ve ha-rachamin be-vina" [Mortality and Mercy in Vienna]. Hebrew translation by Gideon Roury. *Siman Kri' a* 14 (June 1981): 146-57.

D10   Translation by David Albahari of "Entropy." In *Anthology of Contemporary World Stories,* edited by David Albahari. Belgrade, Yugoslavia: Prosveta, 1982. vol. 2.

D11   *Entropy/Entropie: edition bilingue avec notes et postface.* French translation by Martine Claret, D. Grantham, and J. Soonckindt. "Postface" by Louis Soonckindt. Montpellier: Delta Collection Bilingue, 1984.

E. ENDORSEMENTS

BEEN DOWN SO LONG IT LOOKS LIKE UP TO ME / RICHARD FARIÑA

BEEN
DOWN
SO
LONG
IT
LOOKS
LIKE
UP
TO
ME

RICHARD
FARIÑA

RANDOM
HOUSE

It Looks Like Up to Me
THE CLASSIC NOVEL OF THE 1960s
Richard Fariña

Been Down So Long

"It's been a while, since I've read anything quite so groovy, quite such a joy from beginning to end. This book comes on like the Hallelujah Chorus done by 200 kazoo players with perfect pitch, I mean strong, swinging, skilful and reverent—but also with the fine brassy buzz of irreverence in there too. Fariña has going for him an unerring and virtuoso instinct about exactly what, in this bewildering Republic, is serious and what cannot possibly be—and on top of that the honesty to come out and say it straight. In spinning his yarn he spins the reader as well, dizzily into a macrocosm that manages to be hilarious, chilling, sexy, profound, maniacal, beautiful and outrageous all at the same time."
—THOMAS PYNCHON

NEW INTRODUCTION BY
THOMAS PYNCHON

ISBN 0-670-15476-8   VIKING

MY ESCAPE FROM THE CIA (AND OTHER IMPROBABLE EVENTS) RUDD

MY
ESCAPE
FROM
THE CIA
(AND OTHER
IMPROBABLE
EVENTS)
HUGHES
RUDD

WILLIAM STYRON: "At his best, Hughes Rudd is one of the truly gifted and original writers we have."

THOMAS PYNCHON: "You have the feeling, reading these stories, that Hughes Rudd, like some kind of a satanic Santa Claus, is leading you to under the shadow of the great, grotesque American Christmas Tree and over to an assortment of gift packages, each one of which is quietly ticking. The explosions may come while you're reading, or after you've finished a particular story. But it's the thought behind them that really cozy to: to bring you, ready or not, into the presence of truth. Without topping out behind idle metaphors or irrelevant plot devices, Mr. Rudd has succeeded in telling, with all his reporter's force of accuracy, and mastery of detail, and irony, and grace, and sometimes terrifying precision, exactly what the hell having to be an American, now, during years of total war, epidemic anxiety and mass communications whose promise has been corrupted, is really about; where it's really at. He comes as close to the core of the business as anybody has, because he is not only a writer with an enormous genius for spinning a yarn, but also one whose fine ear is tuned both to the reverberations of global history and to the secret whisperings of the human spirit. It is our good luck as readers to share, and certainly to ponder ourselves, the things he has been listening to."

HARVEY SWADOS: "I think he is an original—a keen and rattling short story writer who knows how to get through."

GEORGE PLIMPTON: "These stories are marked by both power and sensibility. Rudd is absolutely first rate—his the equipment of a major writer. I can't imagine that his voice will remain obscure..."

NELSON ALGREN: "Hughes Rudd is the real thing all right. These stories don't have to be read—they whiz by you. He is very fast, always funny, brand new—and so skillful that you don't hear the knockdown roar and the knockdown bellow behind them until after you've closed the book."

40

E1a   Fariña, Richard. *Been Down So Long It Looks Like Up to Me.*
New York: Random House, 1966. Blurb appears on back flap of
dust jacket.

"It's been a while since I've read anything quite so groovy, quite such a joy
from beginning to end. This book comes on like the Hallelujah Chorus
done by 200 kazoo players with perfect pitch, I mean strong, swinging,
skillful and reverent—but also with the fine brassy buzz of irreverence in
there too. Fariña has going for him an unerring and virtuoso instinct about
exactly what, in this bewildering Republic, is serious and what cannot
possibly be—and on top of that the honesty to come out and say it straight.
In spinning his yarn he spins the reader as well, dizzily into a microcosm
that manages to be hilarious, chilling, sexy, profound, maniacal, beautiful
and outrageous all at the same time."

E1b   ———. Shorter version of blurb for full-page ad in *New York Times
Book Review,* 8 May 1966, 9.

E1c   ———. New York: Dell, 1967. First paperback edition. Blurb on
first (unnumbered) page and on back cover.

E1d   ———. New York: Viking/Penguin, 1983. Simultaneous cloth and
paperback editions. Blurb appears on back cover.

E2a   Rudd, Hughes. *My Escape from the CIA (and Other Improbable
Events).* New York: Dutton, 1966. Blurb on back cover of dust
jacket.

"You have the feeling, reading these stories, that Hughes Rudd, like some
kind of a satanic Santa Claus, is leading you in under the shadow of the
great, grotesque American Christmas Tree and over to an assortment of
gift packages, each one of which is quietly ticking. The explosions may
come while you're reading, or after you've finished a particular story. But
it's the thought behind them that really counts: to bring you, ready or not,
into the presence of truth. Without copping out behind idle metaphors or
irrelevant plot devices, Mr. Rudd has succeeded in telling, with all his
reporter's love of accuracy, and mastery of detail, and irony, and grace,
and sometimes terrifying precision, exactly what the hell having to be an
American, now, during years of total war, epidemic anxiety and mass
communications whose promise has been corrupted, is really about; where
it's really at. He comes as close to the core of the business as anybody has,
because he is not only a writer with an enormous genius for spinning a yarn,
but also one whose fine ear is tuned both to the reverberations of global
history and to the secret whisperings of the human spirit. It is our good luck
as readers to share, and certainly to ponder ourselves, the things he has
been listening to."

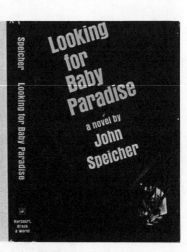

Speicher

Looking for Baby Paradise

Looking for Baby Paradise
a novel by
John Speicher

Harcourt,
Brace
& World

"Revolutionary"

"Watch this Speicher eat, he's a writer of fine and startling talent. His novel is not only funny and frightening, absorbing, compassionate and skillfully-paced, but underneath you can also feel good solid rage, a deep sense of care, and most hopefully a refusal to believe that the world he's telling about really has to be like it is. For reasons Americans have only lately begun looking into, and in the best sense of the word, *Looking for Baby Paradise* is revolutionary." —*Thomas Pynchon*

"Taut and Original"

"I enjoyed this novel enormously. There is humor, sadness, and excitement in this taut and original story of Jewish, Irish, and Puerto Rican kids in a Youth Board Center in upper Manhattan; and there is the frightening reminder that we, like them, are in constant danger from the forces we count to protect us, from the police and the arms, and from the officials who determine when their clubs and guns will be directed against us." —*Joseph Heller*

AVON/V2547/75¢

Be Careful, Man. This Book Is Going To Touch You. It Might Hurt!

Looking For Baby Paradise
by John Speicher

"Watch this Speicher cat, he's a writer of fine and startling talent. His novel is not only funny and frightening, absorbing, compassionate and skillfully-paced, but underneath you can also feel good solid rage, a deep sense of care, and most hopefully a refusal to believe that the world he's telling about really has to be like it is. For reasons Americans have only lately been looking into, and in the best sense of the word, LOOKING FOR BABY PARADISE is revolutionary."
—Thomas Pynchon

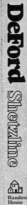

DeFord
Shetzline

DeFord
a novel by
David Shetzline

Random
House

"This is an extraordinary book, quickened by honest rage, written with sustained grace; comic; and impassioned, and always deeply moving; for at its heart is an awareness that the America which should have been is not the America we ourselves live in; that the dissonances set up between the two grow every day wilder and more tragic. What makes Shetzline's voice a truly original and important one is the way he uses these interference-patterns to build his novel, combining an amazing talent for seeing and listening into the shadows and out to the far reaches of the American experience with a yarn-spinner's native gift for picking you up, keeping you in the spell of the action, the chase, not letting go of you till you've said, yes, I see; yes, this is how it is."

—Thomas Pynchon, author of *V* and *The Crying of Lot 49*.

E2b   ———. *My Escape from the CIA (and into CBS)*. New York: Dutton, 1976. First paperback edition, with altered title. Blurb on back cover.

E2c   ———. Shorter version of blurb for ad in *New York Times Book Review,* 2 May 1976, 21.

E3a   Speicher, John. *Looking for Baby Paradise.* New York: Harcourt, Brace & World, 1967. Blurb on back cover of dust jacket.
     Note: blurb also appears on the advance reading copy in orange wrappers.

"Watch this Speicher cat, he's a writer of fine and startling talent. His novel is not only funny and frightening, absorbing, compassionate and skillfully-paced, but underneath you can also feel good solid rage, a deep sense of care, and most hopefully a refusal to believe that the world he's telling about really has to be like it is. For reasons Americans have only lately begun looking into, and in the best sense of the word, *Looking for Baby Paradise* is revolutionary."

E3b   ———. New York: Avon, 1970. First paperback edition. Blurb on front cover.

E3c   ———. Opening line of blurb reprinted on back cover of Speicher's *Didman.* New York: Harper & Row, 1971.

E4   Shetzline, David. *DeFord.* New York: Random House, 1968. Blurb on back cover of dust jacket.

"This is an extraordinary book, quickened by honest rage, written with sustained grace; comic; and impassioned, and always deeply moving; for at its heart is an awareness that the America which should have been is not the America we ourselves live in; that the dissonances set up between the two grow every day wilder and more tragic. What makes Shetzline's voice a truly original and important one is the way he uses these interference-patterns to build his novel, combining an amazing talent for seeing and listening into the shadows and out to the far reaches of the American experience with a yarn-spinner's native gift for picking you up, keeping you in the spell of the action, the chase, not letting go of you till you've said, yes, I see; yes, this is how it is."

E5a   Wurlitzer, Rudolph. *Nog.* New York: Pocket Books, 1970. First paperback edition and the only edition containing the blurb, which appears on the first (unnumbered) page.

"Wow, this is some book, I mean it's more than a beautiful and heavy trip, it's also very important in an evolutionary way, showing us directions we could be moving in—hopefully another sign that the Novel of Bullshit is dead and some kind of re-enlightenment is beginning to arrive, to take hold. Rudolph Wurlitzer is really, really good, and I hope he manages to come down again soon, long enough anyhow to guide us on another one like *Nog.*"

E5b   ———. Blurb reprinted in Dutton's Fall 1970 catalogue, announcing Wurlitzer's second novel *Flats.*

E5c   ———. Shorter version of blurb on back flap of dust jacket of Wurlitzer's *Flats.* New York: Dutton, 1970.

E6a   Piercy, Marge. *Dance the Eagle to Sleep.* Ad in *New York Times Book Review,* 1 November 1970, 55, quoting from a letter by Pynchon to Piercy's publisher.

"It's so good I don't even know how to write a coherent blurb . . . an all-out honest-to-God *novel,* humanity and love hollering from every sentence and the best set of characters since Moby Dick or something."

E6b   ———. Greenwich, Conn.: Fawcett, 1971. First paperback edition and the only edition containing a blurb, apparently from the same letter as above.

"Here is somebody with the guts to go into the deepest core of herself, her time, her history, and risk more than anybody else has so far, just out of a love for the truth and a need to tell it. It's about time."

E6c   ———. Blurb reprinted on front flap of dust jacket of Piercy's *Small Changes.* Garden City, N.Y.: Doubleday, 1973.

E7a   Sale, Kirkpatrick. *SDS.* Shorter version of blurb (see E7b) for ads in *New York Times Book Review,* 6 May 1973, 36, and in *New York Review of Books,* 17 May 1973, 26.

E7b   ———. New York: Vintage Books, 1974. First paperback edition. Blurb on back cover.

"*SDS* is the first great history of the American Prerevolution . . . Because it is a source of clarity, energy and sanity for anyone trying to survive the Nixonian reaction, *SDS* will stand not only on its extraordinary merits, but also as one book that was there when we needed it most."

Their revolution began when their men's ended.

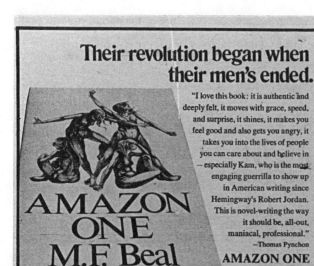

"I love this book: it is authentic and deeply felt, it moves with grace, speed, and surprise, it shines, it makes you feel good and also gets you angry, it takes you into the lives of people you can care about and believe in — especially Kam, who is the most engaging guerrilla to show up in American writing since Hemingway's Robert Jordan. This is novel-writing the way it should be, all-out, maniacal, professional."
—Thomas Pynchon

AMAZON ONE
a novel by the winner of The Atlantic Grant
M.F. Beal

$7.95 at all bookstores
An Atlantic Monthly Press Book
LITTLE, BROWN and COMPANY

#1 NON-FICTION BEST SELLER

Marabel Morgan

The Total Woman

The book that can put the sizzle back in your marriage!

AT YOUR BOOKSTORE
Fleming H. Revell Company
OLD TAPPAN, NEW JERSEY 07675
(If ordering by mail, add 35¢ handling)

---

the Mystery of MAN
by Owen Sharkey

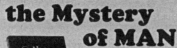

An Anthropologic Study

This very impressive narrative is written from the viewpoint of man's self-awareness and seeks to define man through rational insight.

Sharkey confronts the problematical man and perceives him as an integral part of the whole of reality and therein discovers his true identity.

$10.95 from your bookseller or directly from:

FRANKLIN PUBLISHING COMPANY
2047 Locust Street, Dept. NY
Philadelphia, Pennsylvania 19103

The New York Times Book Review/April 13, 1975

Robert M. Shapiro

"THE KIDS"

It seems that everyone is talking about "the kids." Long hair, strikes, marches, sit-ins, bombings. Why are they so angry? Are they trying to build a city of love out of a nation of garbage? Or just reduce to rubble the only country we've got? Are the recent bombings and killings — in Wisconsin, Boston, New York, Chicago — harbingers of an armed and organized rebellion?

I haven't read any entrails lately, but I have read a hard-driving novel that outlines what might happen the day after tomorrow. Or maybe even tomorrow, DANCE THE EAGLE TO SLEEP tells of four young people who lead the revolt of the young: a rock singer; a red-power "problem student"; a whiz kid exploited by his school; and an army brat who cruises the East Village in search of a new family. Together they organize The Indians, a latter-day tribe of kids from New Rochelle, Shaker Heights, Winnetka, wherever. The Indians develop a national following, nurtured by media headlining 'TEEN GANGS HOLD PAINTED SEX ORGIES' and merchandisers who make capital out of the tribe's lifestyle. But The Indians soon face the inevitable repression in the cities, the communes, even in the forests of the Catskills. It is relentless and brutal and, once again, fully covered by the media, including a daily TV series that blithely chronicles the progress of the Special Forces assigned to wipe out The Indians.

Thomas Pynchon, author of V and The Crying of Lot Forty-Nine, read DANCE THE EAGLE TO SLEEP. His letter came in today. This is what he wrote: "It's so good I don't even know how to write a coherent blurb . . . an all-out honest-to-God novel, humanity and love hollering from every sentence and the best set of characters since Moby Dick or something." That's coherent enough for us, Mr. Pynchon. Thanks.

L.L. Day
Editor-at-Large

DOUBLEDAY PUBLISHES MARGE PIERCY

Dance the Eagle to Sleep ($5.95) is available at all Doubleday Book Shops and other fine book and department stores. Doubleday & Company, Inc., Garden City, New York.

55

E8   Beal, M. F. *Amazon One*. Blurb for ad in *New York Times Book Review,* 13 April 1975, 31. (Not used on book's dust jacket.)

"I love this book: it is authentic and deeply felt, it moves with grace, speed, and surprise, it shines, it makes you feel good and also gets you angry, it takes you into the lives of people you can care about and believe in—especially Kam, who is the most engaging guerilla to show up in American writing since Hemingway's Robert Jordan. This is novel-writing the way it should be, all-out, maniacal, professional."

E9a   Matthiessen, Peter. *Far Tortuga*. New York: Viking, 1975. Blurb on back cover.

"I've enjoyed everything I've ever read by Matthiessen, and this novel is Matthiessen at his best—a masterfully spun yarn, a little otherworldly, a dreamlike momentum . . . It's full of music and strong haunting visuals, and like everything of his, it's also a deep declaration of love for the planet. I wish him and it all kinds of fortune."

E9b   ———. Shorter version of blurb for ad in *New York Times Book Review,* 18 May 1975, 18.

E9c   ———. New York: Bantam, 1976. First paperback edition. Blurb on back cover.

E10a   Robbins, Tom. *Even Cowgirls Get the Blues*. Shorter version of blurb (see E10b) for ad in *New York Times Book Review,* 23 May 1976, 28.

E10b   ———. New York: Bantam, 1977. First mass market paperback edition and the only edition containing the full blurb, which appears on the first (unnumbered) page.

"I did get the advance copy of *Even Cowgirls Get the Blues* but people started borrowing it. 'Gee, this is a great book. How come you haven't read it yet?' Passage of time. Me: 'You're not through with it yet.' 'I'm reading it slow. I don't want it to end.'

"When I finally did get hold of it again, I was prepared to hate it. But ended up loving it and reading it slow because I didn't want it to end. Tom Robbins has a grasp on things that dazzles the brain and he's also a world-class storyteller. This is one of those special novels—a piece of working magic, warm, funny, and sane—that you want to just ride off into the sunset with. Thank you for letting me see it.

"I hope the book sells and sells and winds up changing the brainscape of America, which sure could use it.

"Thanx, pardners."

Book 1: Far Tortuga

Advance Comments on FAR TORTUGA

"With its strange and haunting locations, *Far Tortuga* will certainly point the way that the English-speaking sensibility must and should go, from this book on. It is the way of passionate impressionism. Matthiessen is creating our new vision. A beautiful and moving novel that will not be forgotten by anyone lucky enough to read it."
—James Dickey

"I've enjoyed everything I've ever read by Matthiessen, and this novel is Matthiessen at his best—a masterfully spun yarn, a little otherworldly, a dreamlike momentum . . . It's full of music and strong haunting visuals, and like everything of his, it's also a deep declaration of love for the planet. I wish him and it all kinds of fortune."
—Thomas Pynchon

"Peter Matthiessen's most beautiful book. It goes very deep, with endless subtleties—there's a feeling all the time of its being written by the sea. A wonderful creation."
—Eleanor Clark

"What a tremendous book—the most powerful, most beautiful, and bravest novel in years. He writes brilliantly—moving but unsentimental, tragic but funny as hell, poetic but unmercifully tough. Until I read it, the only novel since World War II that I really wish I'd written was *One Hundred Years of Solitude*; now there are two. I love it so much that I am not even envious, I am exhilarated. I wish Conrad and Melville were alive to read it, and for that matter, Homer."
—Stephen Becker

"A novel about the sea and the wonders below it, and the strange men who have chosen to live or die on a miserable boat hunting for what they know is no longer there. This is an exciting book about important things."
—Lillian Hellman

"A wonderful tone poem about man, the sea and destiny—unique, a real original, and enormously haunting. A work of great beauty that deserves everything."
—William Styron

304-49461-X

FAR TORTUGA
PETER MATTHIESSEN

A NOVEL

RANDOM HOUSE

Book 2: The Pagan Blessing

Dear Phyllis,
Just finished reading The Pagan Blessing, and enjoyed it enormously—in fact, loved it. Not just the writing, which is excellent, but also the feeling, the experience, of reading it. I didn't want your book to end, which usually means I know I'm reading something special. I think you've got a lot going here— the locale, which is fascinating and offbeat, characters who are alive and engaging, a clean up-tempo story line, action, color, comedy, romance—you're right in sync with the "populist" awareness that local is better than centralized, you write about country people without sliding into fake pastoral, and best of all you've celebrated here, magically, the simple power of love. In short, it's a damn good piece of work. Thank you for a delightful, touching, and entertaining journey.
¡Vivan los amantes célticos!

Thomas Pynchon

THE VIKING PRESS · PUBLISHERS · NEW YORK

ISBN 0-670-54012-4

Phyllis Gebauer | THE PAGAN BLESSING | Viking

THE PAGAN BLESSING
A NOVEL BY
Phyllis Gebauer

Book 3: Sounding the Territory

I just read galleys of *Sounding the Territory* by Laurel Goldman. I think it's an astonishing piece of work—I wasn't at all prepared, reading a book full of such laughter and vertigo, to be moved, and touched, as deeply as I was. Laurel Goldman brings to her writing a high-level quality of attention, a demonic sense of humor, a serious respect for life's darkness—it is writing which is able, in the most surely felt way, to enter a reader's heart.

—THOMAS PYNCHON

LAUREL GOLDMAN

304-19455-5

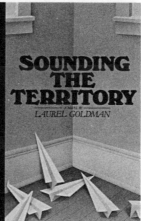

SOUNDING THE TERRITORY
A NOVEL BY
LAUREL GOLDMAN

KNOPF

47

E11a   Gebauer, Phyllis. *The Pagan Blessing.* New York: Viking, 1979. Blurb on back cover.

"Dear Phyllis,
    "Just finished reading The Pagan Blessing, and enjoyed it enormously —in fact, loved it. Not just the writing, which is excellent, but also the feeling, the experience, of reading it. I didn't want your book to end, which usually means I know I'm reading something special. I think you've got a lot going here—the locale, which is fascinating and offbeat, characters who are alive and engaging, a clean up-tempo story line, action, color, comedy, romance—you're right in sync with the 'populist' awareness that local is better than centralized, you write about country people without sliding into fake pastoral, and best of all you've celebrated here, magically, the simple power of love. In short, it's a damn good piece of work. Thank you for a delightful, touching, and entertaining journey.
    "¡Vivan los amantes célticos!"

E11b   ———. Shorter version of blurb for ad in *New York Times Book Review,* 7 October 1979, 28.

E12a   Goldman, Laurel. *Sounding the Territory.* New York: Knopf, 1982. Blurb on back cover.

"I just read galleys of *Sounding the Territory* by Laurel Goldman. I think it's an astonishing piece of work—I wasn't at all prepared, reading a book full of such laughter and vertigo, to be moved, and touched, as deeply as I was. Laurel Goodman brings to her writing a high-level quality of attention, a demonic sense of humor, a serious respect for life's darkness—it is writing which is able, in the most surely felt way, to enter a reader's heart."

E12b   ———. Shorter version of blurb for ad in *New York Times Book Review,* 4 April 1982, 23; repeated in *Village Voice,* "Voice Literary Supplement," 13 April 1982, 12.

E13a   Erickson, Steve. *Days between Stations.* New York: Vintage, 1986. First paperback edition and first to contain blurb, which is on front and back covers.

"Steve Erickson has that rare and luminous gift for reporting back from the nocturnal side of reality, along with an engagingly romantic attitude and the fierce imaginative energy of a born storyteller. It is good news when any of these qualities appear in a writer—to find them all together in a first novelist is reason to break out the champagne and hors-d'oeuvres."

E13b   ———. Shorter version of blurb on back cover of Erickson's *Rubicon Beach.* New York: Vintage, 1987.

"Steve Erickson has that rare and luminous gift for reporting back from the nocturnal side of reality, along with an
engagingly romantic attitude and the fierce imaginative
energy of a born storyteller. It is good news when any
of these qualities appear in a writer—to find them all
together in a first novelist is reason to break out the
champagne and hors-d'œuvres."

— THOMAS PYNCHON

"A fascinating first novel."
— THE PHILADELPHIA INQUIRER

"Steve Erickson is a very impressive talent. His imagination is
boldly cinematic and his ear for the music of language is subtle
and sure."

— RON LOEWINSOHN, author of
MAGNETIC FIELDS

"Erickson is brilliant. Period. Days Between Stations is the novel
of a young writer who could come in range of Thomas Pynchon.
Who might, if he pushed enough, be the kind of writer Norman
Mailer used to refer to as 'major.' He brings love back from
angst and gives it a function."

— MICHAEL VENTURA,
THE LOS ANGELES WEEKLY

Steve Erickson's second novel, Rubicon Beach, is published by
Poseidon Press.

$6.95

Design by Lorraine Louie
Illustration by Rick Lovell

74685

ISBN 0-394-74685-6

VINTAGE
CONTEMPORARIES

Part Two

Secondary Materials

F. BOOKS, ARTICLES, AND CONFERENCE PAPERS

Abádi-Nagy, Zoltán. "The Entropic Rhythm of Thomas Pynchon's Comedy in *The Crying of Lot 49.*" *Hungarian Studies in English* 11 (December 1977): 117-30.

———. "Ironic Historicism in the American Novel of the Sixties." *John O'Hara Journal* 5 (1983): 83-90.

Abernethy, Peter. "Entropy in Pynchon's *The Crying of Lot 49.*" *Critique* 14, no. 2 (1972): 18-33.

Accardo, Annalucia, and Igina Tattoni. "*The Crying of Lot 49* e *Slaughterhouse-Five:* due romanzi contemporanie." *Cultura e Scuola* 22 (1984): 86-98.

Ackroyd, Peter. "Somewhere over the Novel." Review of *Gravity's Rainbow. Spectator,* 17 November 1973, 641-42.

Adams, Michael Vannoy. "The Benzene Uroboros: Plastic and Catastrophe in *Gravity's Rainbow.*" In *Spring 1981: An Annual of Archetypal Psychology & Jungian Thought.* Dallas, Texas: Spring Publications, 1981. 149-61.

Adams, Robert M. "Counterparts." In *AfterJoyce: Studies in Fiction after "Ulysses."* New York: Oxford University Press, 1977. 170-79.

Ahmad, Aijaz. "Jameson's Rhetoric of Otherness and the National Allegory." *Social Text* 7, no. 2 (1987): 3-35.

Akiba, Tsutomu. "On Thomas Pynchon's 'Entropy.' " *Essays and Studies in English Language and Literature* 75 (November 1984): 87-107.

Aldridge, John. "Mere Entropy is Loosed." In *The American Novel and the Way We Live Now.* New York: Oxford University Press, 1983. 65-69.

Allen, Bruce. Review of *Gravity's Rainbow. Library Journal* 98 (1 March 1973): 766.

Allen, Mary. *The Necessary Blankness: Women in Major American Fiction of the Sixties.* Urbana, Illinois: University of Illinois Press, 1976. 37-51.

Alter, Robert. "The Apocalyptic Temper." *Commentary,* June 1966, 61-66.

———. "The New American Novel." *Commentary,* November 1975, 44-51.

———. *Motives for Fiction.* Cambridge: Harvard University Press, 1984. 25-34, 41-42.

Ames, Sanford S. "Pynchon and Visible Language: Ecriture." *International Fiction Review* 4 (1977): 170-73.

———. "Cars 'n Garbage." *Enclitic* 4, no. 1 (Spring 1980): 17-23.

———. Review of Clerc (1983). *International Fiction Review* 11, no. 1 (1984): 68-69.

"American Fiction: The Postwar Years, 1945-1965." *Book Week* (*Sunday Herald Tribune*), 26 September 1965, 1-3, 5-7, 18, 20, 22, 24-25.

Antip, Felicia. "*V.* si V-2." *România Literarâ* 6, no. 20 (1973): 30.

Appel, Alfred, Jr. "An Interview with Vladimir Nabokov." *Wisconsin Studies in Contemporary Literature* 8, no. 2 (Spring 1967): 127-52.

Ashley, Leonard R. N. "Gravity's Rainbow." In *Reference Guide to American Literature,* 2nd ed., edited by D. L. Kirkpatrick. Chicago and London: St. James Press, 1987. 638-39.

Atchity, Kenneth. "Pynchon Reappears with Examples and Apologies." Review of *Slow Learner. Los Angeles Times Book Review,* 6 May 1984, 3.

Babić, Ljiljana. "Pripovetke Tomasa Raglisa Pinčona." *Letopis Matice Srpske* 424 (1979): 1975-80.

Bach, Vella. Review of *The Crying of Lot 49. Perihelion,* October 1982, 1-2.

"Backstage with *Esquire.*" *Esquire,* December 1965, 10.

Baker, John F. "The Awards: High Drama and Low Comedy." *Publishers Weekly,* 13 May 1974, 41-44.

Bakker, J. "The End of Individualism." *Dutch Quarterly Review of Anglo-American Letters* 7 (1977): 286-304.

——. *"Nineteen Eighty-Four* and *Gravity's Rainbow:* Two Anti-Utopias Compared." In *George Orwell,* edited by Courtney T. Wemyss and Alexej Ugrinsky. New York: Greenwood, 1987. 85-91.

Balbert, Peter. "A Panoply of Metaphor: Exuberances of Style in Pynchon and Updike." *Studies in the Novel* 15 (Fall 1983): 265-76.

Baldick, Chris. "Novel Technology." Review of Clerc (1983). *Times Literary Supplement,* 3 June 1983, 576.

Baldwin, Hélène L. "The One Great Centripetal Movement: Empathy in *Gravity's Rainbow." Philological Papers* 31 (1985 [1986]): 116-24.

Balitas, Vincent D. "Charismatic Figures in Thomas Pynchon's *Gravity's Rainbow." Journal of Social Sciences and Humanities* 1, no. 1 (Fall 1977): 2-29. Reprinted abridged in *Pynchon Notes* 9 (June 1982): 38-53.

Balliett, Whitney. "Wha." Review of *V. New Yorker,* 15 June 1963, 113-14, 117.

Ballif, Gene. "Reading, Writing, and Reality." *Salmagundi* 12 (Spring 1970): 25-42.

Banning, Charles Leslie. "William Gaddis' *J R:* The Organization of Chaos and the Chaos of Organization." *Paunch* 42-43 (1975): 153-65.

Banta, Martha. "About America's 'White Terror': James, Poe, Pyncheon [*sic*], and Others." In *Literature and the Occult: Essays in Comparative Literature,* edited by Luanne Frank. Arlington: University of Texas, 1977. 31-53.

Barbedette, Gilles. "Pynchon l'insaisissable." *La Quinzaine littèraire* 499 (31 October 1985): 31-32.

Barth, John. "The Literature of Replenishment: Postmodernist Fiction." *Atlantic Monthly,* January 1980, 65-71. Reprinted in *The Friday Book.* New York: Putnam's, 1984. 193-206.

Bass, Thomas A. *"Gravity's Rainbow* as Orphic Text." *Pynchon Notes* 13 (October 1983): 25-46.

Bassoff, Bruce. "In Search of Narcissus: *The Crying of Lot 49.*" Chap. 4 of *The Secret Sharers: Studies in Contemporary Fiction.* New York: AMS Press, 1983. 49-64.

Batchelor, John Calvin. "Thomas Pynchon Is Not Thomas Pynchon: or, This Is the End of the Plot Which Has No Name." *Soho Weekly News,* 22-28 April 1976, 15-17, 21-35.

———. "Interim Notes: Thomas Pynchon: Real Nowhere Man." *Soho Weekly News,* 29 April-6 May 1976, 16.

———. "The Ghost of Richard Fariña." *Soho Weekly News,* 28 April-4 May 1977, 19-22, 26-27.

Baxter, Charles. Review of Plater (1978). *Criticism* 21, no. 2 (Spring 1979): 179-82.

———. "De-faced America: *The Great Gatsby* and *The Crying of Lot 49.*" *Pynchon Notes* 7 (October 1981): 22-37.

Bayerl, Elizabeth. "Tangled Hierarchies: *Gödel, Escher, Bach* and *Gravity's Rainbow.*" *Pynchon Notes* 10 (October 1982): 52-55.

Baylon, Daniel. "*The Crying of Lot 49:* vrai roman et faux policier?" *Caliban* 23 (1986): 111-25.

Begnal, Michael H. "Thomas Pynchon's *V.:* In Defense of Benny Profane." *Journal of Narrative Technique* 9, no. 2 (Spring 1979): 61-69.

Bell, Pearl K. "Pynchon's Road of Excess." Review of *Gravity's Rainbow. New Leader,* 2 April 1973, 16-17.

Bellman, Samuel Irving. Review of Stark (1980). *Studies in Short Fiction* 18 (Fall 1981): 461-62.

Bengtson, Göran. "Vägen genom *V.*" In *Modern amerikanst prosa,* edited by Jan Broberg. Stockholm: Bo Cavefors, 1968. 159-60.

Bennett, Carl D. "Pynchon, Thomas." In *Encyclopedia of World Literature in the 20th Century,* rev. ed., edited by Leonard S. Klein. New York: Ungar, 1983. 3:610-12.

Bennett, David. "Parody, Postmodernism, and the Politics of Reading." *Critical Quarterly* 27, no. 4 (Winter 1985): 27-43.

Berger, Charles. "Merrill and Pynchon: Our Apocalyptic Scribes." In *James Merrill: Essays in Criticism,* edited by David Lehman and Charles Berger. Ithaca: Cornell University Press, 1983. 282-97. Reprinted in Bloom (1986a): 203-15.

Bergman, Petter. "Hemligt meddelande." In *Modern amerikanst prosa,* edited by Jan Broberg. Stockholm: Bo Cavefors, 1968. 161-63.

Bergonzi, Bernard. *The Situation of the Novel.* Pittsburgh: University of Pittsburgh Press, 1970. 80-83, 91-93, 96-100 and passim.

Bernstein, Jeremy. Individual comments in "Who Reads Novels? A Symposium." *American Scholar* 48, no. 2 (Spring 1979): 165-90.

Berolzheimer, Hobart F. Review of *The Crying of Lot 49. Library Journal* 91 (15 March 1966): 1447.

Berressem, Hanjo. "Godolphin, Goodolphin, Goodol'phin, Goodol'Pyn, Good ol' Pym: A Question of Integration." *Pynchon Notes* 10 (October 1982): 3-17.

———. "A Short Note on Pynchon's Sources for 'The Firm.' " *Pynchon Notes* 15 (Fall 1984): 77-79.

———. "V. in Love: From the 'Other Scene' to the 'New Scene.' " *Pynchon Notes* 18-19 (Spring-Fall 1986): 5-28.

Bertens, Hans. "Het post-modernisme van Thomas Pynchon." *De Gids* 146, no. 6 (1983): 488-95.

Berthoff, Werner. *Fictions and Events: Essays in Criticism and Literary History.* New York: E.P. Dutton, 1971. 106-13.

———. *A Literature Without Qualities: American Writing Since 1945.* Berkeley: University of California Press, 1979. 70-78, 175.

Bessiére, Jean. "Dualite de la nouvelle & du roman: Henry James, Djuna Barnes, Thomas Pynchon." *Palinure* 3 (1987): 28-40.

"The Best and the Brightest." *Book World (Washington Post),* 9 December 1973, 1.

Betts, Richard A. Review of Schaub (1981). *College Literature* 9, no. 1 (Winter 1982): 81-82.

Bischoff, Peter. "Thomas Pynchon, 'Entropy' (1960)." In *Die amerikanische Short Story der Gegenwart: Interpretationen,* edited by Peter Freese. Berlin: Schmidt, 1976. 226-36.

Bishop, E. R. "Pynchon, Thomas." In *Twentieth-Century Science-Fiction Writers,* edited by Curtis C. Smith. New York: St. Martin's, 1981. 436-37.

Black, David. "Pynchon, Brando & the Men's Liberation Movement." Review of *Gravity's Rainbow. Crawdaddy,* October 1973, 87-88.

Black, Joel Dana. "Probing a Post-romantic Paleontology: Thomas Pynchon's *Gravity's Rainbow." Boundary 2* 8 (Winter 1980): 229-54.

———. "The Paper Empires and Empirical Fictions of William Gaddis." *Review of Contemporary Fiction* 2, no. 2 (1982): 22-31.

———. "Pynchon's Eve of De-struction." *Pynchon Notes* 14 (February 1984): 23-38.

———. "Paper Empires of the New World: Pynchon, Gaddis, Fuentes." In *Proceedings of the Xth Congress of the International Comparative Literature Association/Actes du X congrès de l'Association internationale de littérature comparée,* edited by Anna Balakian, et al. New York: Garland, 1985. 68-75.

———. "Postmodernist Fictions: A Review Essay." *Pynchon Notes* 18-19 (Spring-Fall 1986): 96-109.

Blackford, Russell. "Physics and Fantasy: Scientific Mysticism, Kurt Vonnegut and *Gravity's Rainbow." Journal of Popular Culture* 19, no. 3 (1985): 35-44.

Bloom, Harold, ed. *Thomas Pynchon: Modern Critical Views.* New York: Chelsea House, 1986[a].

———. *Thomas Pynchon's "Gravity's Rainbow": Modern Critical Interpretations.* New York: Chelsea House, 1986[b].

———. "Introduction." In *Norman Mailer: Modern Critical Views.* New York: Chelsea House, 1986. 1-6.

———. "Thomas Pynchon." In *Twentieth-Century American Literature.* 7 vols. New York: Chelsea House, 1985-88. 6:3252-3301.

————. [See under Spirer, Ellen.]

Boef, August Hans den. "Thomas Pynchon." *Dietsche Warande en Belfort: Tijdschrift voor Letterkunde en Geestesleven* 130 (October 1985): 592-98.

Boheemen-Saaf, Christel van. "The Artist as Con Man: The Reaction against the Symbolist Aesthetic in Recent American Fiction." *Dutch Quarterly Review of Anglo-American Letters* 7 (1977): 305-18.

"Book Ends." *New York Times Book Review,* 4 May 1975, 61.

Bowman, John S. "The Agony and the Entropy." *Harvard Magazine* 81, no. 2 (November-December 1978): 14-16.

Bradbury, Malcolm. *The Modern American Novel.* New York: Oxford University Press, 1983. 156-57, 161, 163, 174-79, 180.

————. "The Invisible Man." Review of *Slow Learner. Observer,* 13 January 1985, 51.

Brashear de Gonzáles, Ann. "La novela totalizadora: Pynchon's *Gravity's Rainbow* and Fuentes' *Terra Nostra.*" *Kañina* 5, no. 2 (July-December 1981): 99-106.

Braudy, Leo. "Providence, Paranoia, and the Novel." *ELH* 48 (Fall 1981): 619-37.

Brewer, Maria Minich. "Surviving Fictions: Gender and Difference in Postmodern and Postnuclear Narrative." *Discourse* 9 (1987): 37-52 (42, 43).

Brier, Peter A. "Caliban Reigns: Romantic Theory and Some Contemporary Fantasists." *Denver Quarterly* 13 (Spring 1978): 38-51.

Brigg, Peter. "*Gravity's Rainbow.*" In *Survey of Science Fiction Literature,* edited by Frank N. Magill. Englewood Cliffs, New Jersey: Salem Press, 1979. 2:915-20.

Brivic, Sheldon. Review of Slade (1974). *Journal of Modern Literature* 5 (1976): 791-92.

————. Review of Levine and Leverenz (1976). *Journal of Modern Literature* 6 (1977): 704-5.

———. Review of Plater (1978) and Siegel (1978). *Journal of Modern Literature* 7 (1979): 800-802.

———. Review of Cowart (1980) and Stark (1980). *Journal of Modern Literature* 8 (1980-81): 599-600.

———. Review of Fowler (1980) and Schaub (1981). *Journal of Modern Literature* 9 (December 1982): 520-22.

Brodin, Pierre. "Thomas Pynchon." *Ecrivains américains d'aujourd' hui: des années 60.* Paris: Debresse, 1969. 201-9.

Brooke-Rose, Christine. "Where Do We Go from Here?" *Granta* 3 (1980): 161-88.

———. *A Rhetoric of the Unreal: Studies in Narrative Structure, Especially of the Fantastic.* Cambridge: Cambridge University Press, 1981. 367-70 and passim.

Brosnahan, John. Review of *Slow Learner. Booklist* 80 (15 April 1984): 1129.

Brugiére, Marion. "Les Avatars de la quête dans *The Crying of Lot 49* de Thomas Pynchon." *Delta* 8 (1979): 143-54. Translated by Margaret Langford as "Quest Avatars in Thomas Pynchon's *The Crying of Lot 49.*" *Pynchon Notes* 9 (June 1982): 5-16.

Brunner, John. "Coming Events: An Assessment of Thomas Pynchon's *Gravity's Rainbow." Foundation* 10 (1976): 20-27.

Brunvand, Jan H. "Alligators in the Sewers." *The Vanishing Hitch Hiker: American Urban Legends and Their Meanings.* New York: Norton, 1981. 90-101.

Bryant, Jerry H. *The Open Decision: The Contemporary American Novel and Its Intellectual Background.* New York: The Free Press, 1970. 9, 35-36, 40, 249, 252-57.

Bryfonski, Dedria, ed. *Contemporary Literary Criticism: Excerpts from Criticism of the Works of Today's Novelists, Poets, Playwrights, and Other Creative Writers.* Detroit: Gale Research, 1978. 9:442-47.

———. *Contemporary Literary Criticism: Excerpts from Criticism of the Works of Today's Novelists, Poets, Playwrights, and Other Creative*

Writers. Detroit: Gale Research, 1979. 11:452-57.

Buckeye, Robert. "The Anatomy of the Psychic Novel." *Critique* 9, no. 2 (1967): 33-45.

Bulgheroni, Marisa. "Quattro romanzieri in casa Usher." Final chapter of *Il Demone del luogo: letture americane*. Milan: Instituto Editorale Cisalpino, 1968. 129-33.

Bunster, Elizabeth. "Autumn Books: What to Look Out For." Review of *Slow Learner. Books and Bookmen,* September 1984, 33.

Burgess, Anthony. *99 Novels: The Best in English Since 1939*. New York: Summit, 1984. 109.

Burrows, Miles. "Paranoid Quests." Review of *The Crying of Lot 49. New Statesman,* 14 April 1967, 513-14.

Busch, Frederick. "The Friction of Fiction: A *Ulysses* Omnirandum." *Chicago Review* 26, no. 4 (1975): 5-17.

Byrd, Scott. "A Separate War: Camp and Black Humor in Recent American Fiction." *Language Quarterly* 7, no. 1-2 (Fall-Winter 1968): 7-10.

Caesar, Terry P. "A Note on Pynchon's Naming." *Pynchon Notes* 5 (February 1981): 5-10.

———. "Recent American Fiction." *Pynchon Notes* 10 (October 1982): 45-51.

———. " 'Trapped inside Their frame with your wastes piling up': Mindless Pleasures in *Gravity's Rainbow." Pynchon Notes* 14 (February 1984): 39-48.

———. "Pynchon in China." *Pynchon Notes* 15 (Fall 1984): 47-57.

———. " 'Beasts Vaulting Among the Earthworks': Monstrosity in *Gravity's Rainbow." Novel* 17 (Winter 1984): 158-70.

Cain, Jimmie E., Jr. "The Clock as Metaphor in 'Mondaugen's Story.' " *Pynchon Notes* 17 (Fall 1985): 73-77.

Calhoun, John C. "The Concept of Revolution and Its Influence on the Genesis of Art in the Work of Thomas Pynchon." *Perspectives on Contemporary Literature* 2, no. 1 (1976): 40-52.

Calendrillo, Linda. "Cloaks and More Cloaks: Pynchon's *V.* and the Classic Spy Novel." *Clues* 5, no. 2 (Fall-Winter 1984): 58-65. Published version of paper presented at the Midwest Popular Culture Conference. Columbus, Ohio, 22-24 October 1981.

Callens, Johan. "Reading Pynchon into the Eighties." *Dutch Quarterly Review* 13, no. 2 (1983): 103-19.

———. Review of Schaub (1981). *Revue belge de philologie et d'histoire* 61 (1983): 715-18.

Callow, Phillip. "All Agog." Review of *The Crying of Lot 49. Books and Bookmen,* June 1967, 20.

Carboni, Guido. "La Finzione necessaria: considerazioni sulla postmodern fiction negli USA." *Calibano* 7 (1982): 58-85 (74-77).

Carpenter, Richard C. "State of Mind: The California Setting of *The Crying of Lot 49.*" In *Essays on California Writers,* edited by Charles L. Crow. Bowling Green, Ohio: Bowling Green University Press, 1977. 105-13.

Carter, Dale. *The Final Frontier: The Rise and Fall of the American Rocket State.* London: Verso, 1988.

Cassola, Arnold. "Pynchon, *V.,* and the Malta Connection." *Journal of Modern Literature* 12 (June 1985): 311-31.

Chaffee, Patricia. "The Whale and the Rocket: Technology as Sacred Symbol." *Renascence* 32 (Spring 1980): 146-51.

"Christmas Books." *New York Times Book Review,* 2 December 1973, vii, 1.

Cieński, Marcin. "Rytualy Thomasa Pynchona." *Literatura na Świecie* 7/168 (1985): 196-209.

Claas, Dietmar. " 'Ein abgekartetes Spiel?' Handlungsspiele in *Die Versteigerung von No. 49* und die innovative Leistung des Lesers." In Ickstadt (1981), 128-46.

———. "Die Dynamik der Zwischenräume-endzeitstrategien bei Pynchon." In *Entgrenztes Spiel: Leserhandlungen in der postmodernen amerikanischen Erzählkunst.* Stuttgart: Franz Steiner Verlag, Wiesbaden GmbH, 1984. 78-119.

Clark, Beverly Lyon. Review of Stark (1980) and Mackey (1980). *Modern Fiction Studies* 27 (Summer 1981): 379-80.

———. Review of Schaub (1981). *Studies in American Fiction* 10 (1982): 120-21.

———. "Of Rockets and Sprockets, History and Mystery, Philology and Technology." Review of Clerc (1983). *Pynchon Notes* 12 (June 1983): 48-51.

———. "Realizing *Gravity's* Fantasy." *Pynchon Notes* 17 (Fall 1985): 15-34.

———. "Pynchon: Ones and Zeroes." Chap. 6 of *Reflections of Fantasy: The Mirror-Worlds of Carroll, Nabokov, and Pynchon.* New York: Peter Lang, 1986. 113-42.

———, and Caryn Fuoroli. "A Review of Major Pynchon Criticism." In Pearce (1981), 230-54.

Clark, Roger. "Imperialism in *Gravity's Rainbow.*" *USF Language Quarterly* 21, no. 1-2 (Fall-Winter 1982): 38. Published version of lecture originally given at CEA Conference on "Teaching Pynchon to Undergraduates," 3 April 1981.

Clemons, Walter. "The Sky's the Limit." Review of *Gravity's Rainbow. Newsweek,* 19 March 1973, 92-94.

Clerc, Charles. "Film in *Gravity's Rainbow.*" In Clerc (1983), 103-51.

———, ed. *Approaches to "Gravity's Rainbow."* Columbus, Ohio: Ohio State University Press, 1983.

Coates, Paul. *The Realist Fantasy: Fiction and Reality Since "Clarissa."* New York: St. Martin's, 1983. 12-15, 193-217, and passim.

———. "Unfinished Business: Thomas Pynchon and the Quest for Revolution." *New Left Review* 160 (November-December 1986): 122-28.

Cocks, Geoffrey. "War, Man, and Gravity: Thomas Pynchon and Science Fiction." *Extrapolation* 20 (Winter 1979): 368-77.

Cohen, Jonathan. "Pynchon Forsakes Silence." *Cornell Daily Sun*, 4 November 1977, 9.

Coleman, Loren. "Alligators-in-the-Sewers: A Journalistic Origin." *Journal of American Folklore* 92 (1979): 335-38.

Colville, Georgiana M. "L'Alchimie de Pynchon dans *The Crying of Lot 49*." *Recherches anglaises et américaines* 17 (1984): 213-18.

———. "Ville dans la brume: Perspectives littéraires de San Francisco." *Recherches anglaises et américaines* 18 (1985): 299-313.

———. *Beyond and beneath the Mantle: On Thomas Pynchon's "The Crying of Lot 49."* Amsterdam: Rodopi, 1988.

Comnes, Judith and Gregory. "Physics of Fiction." Paper presented at the 1988 Conference of the Society for Literature & Science. Albany, New York, 6-9 October 1988.

Cook, Bruce. "New Pynchon: Take-Over or Con Job?" *National Observer*, 17 March 1973, 23.

Cook, Don L. Review of Hite (1983). *American Literature* 56 (December 1984): 625-27.

Cooper, Peter. *Signs and Symptoms: Thomas Pynchon and the Contemporary World.* Berkeley: University of California Press, 1983.

Corker, David. Biographical sketch in *Makers of Modern Culture*, edited by Justin Wintle. London: Routledge & Kegan Paul, 1981. 427.

Cosenza, Joseph A. "Reader-Baiting in *Gravity's Rainbow*." *Massachusetts Studies in English* 9, no. 1 (1983): 44-53.

Couturier, Maurice. "The Death of the Real in *The Crying of Lot 49*." *Direction de travail: Agregation d'Anglais 410.* Draguignan: C.N.E.C./ Ministere de l'Education nationale, [1985].

———. "'Do I Know You?' Author-Reader Relationship in *The Crying of Lot 49*." *Cycnos* [Nice, France] 2 (Winter 1985-86): 121-34.

————. "Yours faithfully, the Author." In *Critical Angles: European Views of Contemporary American Literature,* edited by Marc Chénetier. Carbondale: Southern Illinois University Press, 1986. 29-44.

Cowart, David. "Pynchon's *The Crying of Lot 49* and the Paintings of Remedios Varo." *Critique* 18, no. 3 (1977): 19-26.

————. "Love and Death: Variations on a Theme in Pynchon's Early Fiction." *Journal of Narrative Technique* 7, no. 3 (1977): 157-69.

————. "Cinematic Auguries of the Third Reich in *Gravity's Rainbow.*" *Literature/Film Quarterly* 6 (1978): 364-70.

————. " 'Sacrificial Ape': King Kong and His Antitypes in *Gravity's Rainbow.*" *Literature and Psychology* 28, no. 3-4 (1978): 112-18.

————. "Pynchon's Use of the Tannhäuser-Legend in *Gravity's Rainbow.*" *Notes on Contemporary Literature* 9, no. 3 (1979): 2-3.

————. Review of Mendelson (1978). *Journal of Aesthetic Education* 13, no. 3 (1979): 125-27.

————. "V. in Florence: Botticelli's *Birth of Venus* and the Metamorphosis of Victoria Wren." *Southern Humanities Review* 13 (1979): 345-53.

————. *Thomas Pynchon: The Art of Allusion.* Carbondale: Southern Illinois University Press, 1980; London: Feffer, 1980.

————. "Science and the Arts in Pynchon's *Entropy.*" *CLA Journal* 24, no. 1 (1980): 108-15.

————. "Baedeker to Pynchon." *Pynchon Notes* 5 (February 1981): 20-27.

————. Review of Schaub (1981). *Journal of English and Germanic Philology* 81 (April 1982): 285-87.

————. "Thomas Pynchon." In *Critical Survey of Long Fiction: English Language Series,* edited by Frank N. Magill. Englewood Cliffs, New Jersey: Salem Press, 1983. 6:2186-94.

————. Review essay of *Slow Learner* in *Magill's Literary Annual 1985: Essay-Reviews of 200 Outstanding Books Published in the United States During 1984.* Englewood Cliffs, New Jersey: Salem Press, 1985. 830-34.

Cox, Stephen D. "Berkeley, Blake, and the Apocalypse of Pynchon's *The Crying of Lot 49." Essays in Literature* 7, no. 1 (Spring 1980): 91-99.

Crews, Frederick C. "They're Mannerists, Not Moralists." *Book Week Paperback Issue,* 10 January 1965, 5, 27.

Crow, John. "History and Destiny: Problems of Continuity in Pynchon and LeGuin." Paper presented at the Popular Culture Association, April 1979.

Cullen, Robert J. "Pynchon at the MLA Convention." *Pynchon Notes* 11 (February 1983): 3-5.

Cummins, Walter. "Inventing Memories: Apocalyptics and Domestics." *Literary Review* 23 (1980): 127-33.

Curley, Dorothy Nyren, Maurice Kramer, and Elaine Fialka Kramer, eds. *A Library of Literary Criticism: Modern American Literature.* 4th ed. New York: Frederick Ungar, 1969. 3:35-38.

Currie, Peter. "The Eccentric Self: Anti-Characterization and the Problem of the Subject in American Postmodernist Fiction." In *Contemporary American Fiction,* edited by Malcolm Bradbury and Sigmund Ro. London: Edward Arnold, 1987. 60-66.

Dahiya, Bhim. "Structural Patterns in the Novels of Barth, Vonnegut and Pynchon." *Indian Journal of American Studies* 5, no. 1-2 (1976): 53-68.

D'Amico, Maria Vittona. "A Transmarginal Reading of *Gravity's Rainbow." Anuario* [Barcelona] (1980): 17-32.

———. "Thomas Pynchon." In *Novecento americano,* edited by Elemire Zolla. Rome: Lucarini, 1981. 545-59.

Daniel, John. "Quest for Identity." Review of *V. Manchester Guardian Weekly,* 17 October 1963, 11.

Darabaner, Richard. "A Possible Source for the Title of 'The Small Rain.'" *Pynchon Notes* 15 (Fall 1984): 69-72.

Davidson, Cathy N. "Oedipa as Androgyne in Thomas Pynchon's *The Crying of Lot 49.*" *Contemporary Literature* 18 (Winter 1977): 38-50.

Davis, Douglas M. "The New Mood: An Obsession with the Absurd." *National Observer,* February 1965, 22.

Davis, Joann. "Corlies Smith at the Helm." *Publishers Weekly,* 12 April 1985, 46-47.

Davis, Robert M. "The Shrinking Garden and New Exits: The Comic-Satiric Novel in the Twentieth Century." *Kansas Quarterly* 1, no. 3 (1969): 5-16.

———. "Parody, Paranoia, and the Dead End of Language in 2The Crying of Lot 49." *Genre* 4 (December 1972): 367-77.

Daw, Laurence. "The Asymmetry of Life in *Gravity's Rainbow.*" *Pynchon Notes* 9 (June 1982): 66-68.

———. "The Ellipsis as Architectonic in *Gravity's Rainbow.*" *Pynchon Notes* 11 (February 1983): 54-56.

———. "More on Pynchon on Record." *Pynchon Notes* 12 (June 1983): 46-47.

———. "The Limitations of Indeterminancy in Pynchon's Fiction." *CEA Critic* 49, no. 2-4 (Winter 1986-Summer 1987): 174-79.

De Feo, Ronald. Review of *Gravity's Rainbow. Hudson Review* 26 (Winter 1973-74): 773-75.

Delany, Samuel R. "The Semiology of Silence." Interview by Sinda Gregory and Larry McCaffery. *Science Fiction Studies* 14, no. 2 (1987): 134-64 (147, 153). Reprinted in McCaffery and Gregory's *Alive and Writing: Interviews with American Authors of the 1980s.* Urbana: University of Illinois Press, 1987.

Delbourg, Patrice. "Gai comme un Pynchon." Review of *Vente à la criée du lot 49. Nouvelle Observer,* 6 February 1987.

De Paul, Stephen. "Plastic and the Parabola: The New Vocabulary of Attention in Pynchon's *Gravity's Rainbow.*" *CEA Critic* 49, no. 2-4 (Winter 1986-Summer 1987): 180-84.

De Vore, Lynn. "In the Zone: Pynchon and Vietnam." Paper presented at the Midwest Popular Culture Conference. Columbus, Ohio, 22-24 October 1981.

Dick, Bernard F. "At the Crossroads of Time: Types of Simultaneity in Literature and Film." *Georgia Review* 33 (Summer 1979): 423-32.

Dickstein, Morris. "Black Humor and History: Fiction in the Sixties." *Partisan Review* 43 (1976): 185-211.

Dillard, R.H.W. Review of *V.* in *Survey of Contemporary Literature,* rev. ed., edited by Frank N. Magill. Englewood Cliffs, New Jersey: Salem Press, 1977. 12:7955-57.

DiPiero, William S. "*Gravity's Rainbow* come anti-entropia." *Paragone* 302 (April 1975): 105-8.

Dobbs, Kildare. Review of *V. Tamarack Review* 8 (Summer 1963): 92-93.

Doherty, Paul C. "The Year's Best in Paperbacks." *America* 130, no. 5 (9 February 1974): 93-94.

Donadio, Stephen. "America, America." Review of *The Crying of Lot 49.* *Partisan Review* 33 (Summer 1966): 448-52.

Dudar, Helen. "Lifting the Veil on the Life of a Literary Recluse." *Chicago Tribune Bookworld,* 8 April 1984; sec. 14, 35-36. Reprinted as "A Pynchon for Privacy," *Newsday,* 9 April 1984, part II, 3; reprinted as "Pynchon: Early Tales from a Private Man," *Philadelphia Inquirer,* 16 April 1984, 1-E; reprinted as "Pynchon: The Man Who Won't Come to Dinner," *Los Angeles Times,* 22 April 1984, Calendar Section: 6.

Dugdale, John. " 'A Burglar, I Think. A Second-story Man.' " Review of *Slow Learner. Cambridge Quarterly* 15 (1986): 156-64.

Durand, Régis. "On *Aphanisis:* A Note on the Dramaturgy of the Subject in Narrative Analysis." *MLN* 98 (1983): 860-70. Reprinted in French as "De *l'aphanisis:* Notes sur la question du sujet dans le texte contemporain" in *Passage du temps, ordre de la transition,* edited by Jean Bessière. Paris: Picardie Universite de France, 1985. 83-89.

Duyfhuizen, Bernard. "A Brief Further Remark on 'Pynchon's Anti-Quests.' " *Pynchon Notes* 4 (October 1980): 25.

———. "A Long View of V-2." *Pynchon Notes* 5 (February 1981): 17-19.

———. "Starry-Eyed Semiotics: Learning to Read Slothrop's Map and *Gravity's Rainbow.*" *Pynchon Notes* 6 (June 1981): 5-33.

———. "Pynchon Anthologized." Review of *The Crying of Lot 49* in Richter's *Forms of the Novella. Pynchon Notes* 9 (June 1982): 69-72.

———. Review of Schaub (1981): *Journal of American Studies* 16 (1982): 314-15.

———. Review of Clerc (1983). *Modern Fiction Studies* 29 (1983): 741-44.

———. Review of Cooper (1983). *American Literature* 55 (December 1983): 664-66.

———. Introduction to "Deconstructing *Gravity's Rainbow.*" *Pynchon Notes* 14 (February 1984): 3-6.

———. "Included Middles and the Trope of the Absent Insight." Review of Hite (1983). *Pynchon Notes* 14 (February 1984): 75-81.

Dziedzic, Piotr. "Rekonstruowanie Thomasa Pynchona, czyli paranoja kontrolowana." In *Literatura na Świecie* 7/168 (1985): 270-79.

Earl, James. "Scientific and Philosophical Themes in *Gravity's Rainbow.*" American Literature Seminar 268, MLA Convention. San Francisco, 28 December 1975.

———. "Freedom and Knowledge in the Zone." In Clerc (1983), 229-50.

"Eclectic Reading." *New York Times,* 20 April 1974, 30.

Eddins, Dwight. "Paradigms Reclaimed: The Language of Science in *Gravity's Rainbow.*" *Markham Review* 12, no. 4 (Summer 1983): 77-80.

———. "Orphic contra Gnostic: Religious Conflict in *Gravity's Rainbow.*" *Modern Language Quarterly* 45 (June 1984): 163-90.

Edinborough, Arnold. "Random Harvest." Review of *The Crying of Lot 49*. *Saturday Night,* August 1966, 25-26.

Edwards, Brian. "Thomas Pynchon's Myth-Making: A Reading of *Gravity's Rainbow*." In *American Studies: New Essays from Australia and New Zealand,* edited by Roger J. Bell and Ian J. Bickerton. Kensington: Australian and New Zealand American Studies Association, 1981. 26-39.

————. "Mixing Media: Film as Metaphor in Pynchon's *Gravity's Rainbow*." *Australian Journal of American Studies* 1, no. 3 (July 1982): 1-15.

Elliott, George P. "Fiction and Anti-Fiction." *American Scholar* 47 (Summer 1978): 398-406.

Ellis, Reuben J. "King Ludd Sets up Shop in the Zone: Narrator as Trickster in *Gravity's Rainbow*." *Pynchon Notes* 18-19 (Spring-Fall 1986): 66-83.

Ellison, Harlan. Interviewed by David Cowart as part of biographical profile. In *Contemporary Authors, New Revision Series,* edited by Ann Evory. Detroit: Gale Research, 1982. 5:168-75.

Ethridge, James M., Barbara Kopala, and Carolyn Riley, eds. *Contemporary Authors: A Bio-Bibliographical Guide to Current Authors and Their Works.* Detroit: Gale Research, 1968. 19/20: 352-54.

Fahy, Joseph. "Thomas Pynchon's *V.* and Mythology." *Critique* 18, no. 3 (1977): 5-18.

Fariña, Richard. "The Monterey Fair." *Mademoiselle,* March 1964; reprinted in *Long Time Coming and a Long Time Gone.* New York: Random House, 1969. 135-54.

"Faulkner Novel Award Given." *New York Times,* 3 February 1964, 25.

Feeney, Mark. "Pynchon Short Stories Show the Master as Apprentice." Review of *Slow Learner. Boston Sunday Globe,* 1 April 1984, B11, 13.

Feldman, Burton. "Anatomy of Black Humor." *Dissent* 15 (1968): 158-60.

Reprinted in *The American Novel Since World War II,* edited by Marcus Klein. Greenwich, Connecticut: Fawcett, 1969. 224-28.

Feldman, Irving. "Keeping Cool." Review of *V. Commentary* 36 (September 1963): 258-60.

Fiedler, Leslie A. "Literature and Lucre: A Meditation." *Genre* 13, no. 1 (1980): 1-10.

Finney, Michael. " 'Shit 'n Shinola': Obscurity in *Finnegans Wake* and *Gravity's Rainbow."* American Literature Special Session 388, MLA convention. New York, 28 December 1976.

Fiorelli, Edward. *"The Crying of Lot 49."* In *Masterplots II: American Fiction Series,* edited by Frank N. Magill. Englewood Cliffs, New Jersey: Salem Press, 1986. 1:361-65.

Fleischmann, Louisa, and Burt Weinshanker. "Pynchon Enters the Zone, or: Almost Lost in Translation?" Review of Ickstadt (1981). *Pynchon Notes* 8 (February 1982): 54-60.

Fletcher, M. D. "Pynchon's *The Crying of Lot 49:* Postmodern Apologue." Chap. 6 of *Contemporary Political Satire: Narrative Strategies in the Postmodern Context.* Lanham, Maryland: University Press of America, 1987. 113-36.

Fogel, Jean-François. "L'ecrivain invisible: la piste Pynchon." *Libèration,* n.s. no. 1367 (11 October 1985): 30-33.

Fogel, Stanley. *"The Investigation:* Stanislaw Lem's Pynchonesque Novel." *Riverside Quarterly* 6, no. 4 (1977): 286-89. Reprinted in *Riverside Quarterly* 7, no. 2 (1982): 123-26.

———. "Gobble, Gobble, Gobble: Critical Appetites." Review of Clerc (1983) and others. *Canadian Review of American Studies* 15 (1984): 487-96.

———. " 'Everybody Must Get Stoned': Reading Thomas Pynchon." In *The Postmodern University: Essays on the Deconstruction of the Humanities.* Toronto: ECW Press, 1988. 88-105.

Fowler, Douglas. "Pynchon's Magic World." *South Atlantic Quarterly* 79, no. 1 (Winter 1980): 51-60.

———. *A Reader's Guide to Pynchon's "Gravity's Rainbow."* Ann Arbor, Michigan: Ardis Publications, 1980.

———. "Story into Chapter: Thomas Pynchon's Transformation of 'Under the Rose.' " *Journal of Narrative Technique* 14, no. 1 (1984): 33-34.

———. "Epilepsy as Metaphor in *The Crying of Lot 49.*" *Notes on Contemporary Literature* 14, no. 2 (1984): 10-12.

———. *A Reader's Guide to Thomas Pynchon's "The Crying of Lot 49."* Santa Barbara, California: Kinko's, 1986.

Fremont-Smith, Eliot. "Nature—Human and Mother." *New York,* 29 April 1974, 75.

French, Warren. Review of McConnell's *Four Postwar American Novelists. American Literature* 49 (January 1978): 672-74.

Friedbichler, Michael. "Toward a Redeemed Imagination: the Role of Paranoia in the Novels of Thomas Pynchon." In *Forms of the American Imagination: Beiträge zur neueren amerikanischen Literatur,* edited by Arno Heller, et al. Innsbruck: Institut für Sprachwissenschaft der Universität Innsbruck, 1979. 147-56.

Friedman, Alan J. "The Novelist and Modern Physics: New Metaphors for Traditional Themes." *Journal of College Science Teaching* 4 (1975): 310-12.

———. "Science and Technology." In Clerc (1983), 69-102.

——— and Manfred Pütz. "Science as Metaphor: Thomas Pynchon and *Gravity's Rainbow.*" *Contemporary Literature* 15 (Summer 1974): 345-59. Reprinted in Pearce (1981), 69-81. Reprinted as *"Gravity's Rainbow:* Science as Metaphor" in Bloom (1986a), 23-35.

Friedman, Bruce Jay. "Foreword." In *Black Humor: A Unique Anthology Including Works by Pynchon, Knickerbocker, Donleavy, Purdy, Simmons, Rechy, Heller, Barth, Céline, Albee, Southern,* edited by Friedman. New York: Bantam Books, 1965. vii-xi. Reprinted in *The Sense of the Sixties,* edited by Edward Quinn and Paul J. Dolan. New York: The Free Press, 1968. 435-39.

Friedman, Melvin J. "To Make It New: The American Novel Since 1945." *Wilson Quarterly* 2, no. 1 (Winter 1978): 133-78.

——. "The Schlemiel: Jew and Non-Jew." *Studies in the Literary Imagination* 9, no. 1 (Spring 1976): 139-53.

Fry, August J. "The Clouding of the Wine: Reading Thomas Pynchon's *The Crying of Lot 49.*" In *Essays on English and American Literature and a Sheaf of Poems,* edited by J. Bakker et al. Amsterdam: Rodopi, 1987. 143-49.

Frye, Northrop. *Divisions on a Ground: Essays on Canadian Culture,* edited by James Polk. Toronto: Anansi, 1982. 17-18, 186.

Fussell, Paul. "Persistence and Memory: The Ritual of Military Memory." In *The Great War and Modern Memory.* New York: Oxford University Press, 1975. 328-34. Reprinted as "The Brigadier Remembers" (editor's title) in Mendelson (1978), 213-19. Reprinted as "The Ritual of Military Memory" in Bloom (1986b), 21-27.

——. "Within the Conventions." *Spectator,* 29 October 1977, 20-21.

Gaines, Ervin J. Review of *V. Library Journal* 88 (15 February 1963): 795-96.

Gallo, Louis. "Slothrop's Progress: The Fragmented Pilgrim." American Literature Session 703, MLA Convention. Chicago, 30 December 1977.

Galloway, David D. "Milk and Honey." Review of *The Crying of Lot 49. Spectator,* 14 April 1967, 425-26.

Ganz, Earl. "Pynchon in Hiding." *Plum* 3 (1980): 5-20.

Gardner, John. *On Moral Fiction.* New York: Basic Books, 1978. 93-94, 130, 195-96.

Garfitt, Roger. "Safe Audacity." *Listener,* 15 November 1973, 674-75.

Gary, Romain. "To the Editor." *New York Times Book Review,* 12 June 1966, 35.

"A Gathering of Favorites." *Book Week,* 4 December 1966, 4, 36.

Geeslin, Campbell. Review of *Slow Learner. People,* 14 May 1984, 11.

Gelfant, Blanche. "Sister to Faust: The City's 'Hungry Woman' as Heroine." *Novel* 15 (1981): 23-38.

Gentry, Curt. "The Quest for the Female Named V." Review of *V. San Francisco Sunday Chronicle,* 19 May 1963, 17.

George, N. F. "The *Chymische Hochzeit* of Thomas Pynchon." *Pynchon Notes* 4 (October 1980): 5-22.

Gerstenberger, Donna, and George Hendrick. "Pynchon, Thomas." In *The American Novel: A Checklist of Twentieth Century Criticism on Novels Written Since 1789.* Volume II: Criticism Written 1960-1968. Chicago: Swallow, 1970. 297.

Gilbert-Rolfe, Jeremy, and John Johnston. "*Gravity's Rainbow* and the Spiral Jetty." *October* 1, no. 1 (Spring 1976): 65-85; 1, no. 2 (Summer 1976): 71-90; 1, no. 3 (Autumn 1976): 90-102.

Glicksberg, Charles I. "Experimental Fiction: Innovation versus Form." *Centennial Review* 18, no. 2 (Spring 1974): 127-50.

Gold, Arthur R. "Like a Yo-Yo, Spinning through a Dehumanized Age." Review of *V. New York Herald Tribune Books,* 21 April 1963, 3.

———. "A Mad Dash after an Unholy Grail." Review of *The Crying of Lot 49. Book Week,* 24 April 1966, 5.

Golden, Robert E. "Mass Man and Modernism: Violence in Pynchon's *V.*" *Critique* 14, no. 2 (1972): 5-17.

Goldstein, Laurence. "Thomas Pynchon's *Gravity's Rainbow.*" In *The Flying Machine and Modern Literature.* Bloomington: Indiana University Press, 1986. 180-85.

Goolrick, Robert Cooke. "Pieces of Pynchon." *New Times,* 16 October 1978, 59-70.

Grace, Sherrill E. "Wastelands and Badlands: The Legacies of Pynchon and Kroetsch." *Mosaic* 14, no. 2 (Spring 1981): 21-34.

———. *The Voyage That Never Ends: Malcolm Lowry's Fiction.* Vancouver: University of British Columbia Press, 1982. 121-22.

————. "Fritz Lang and the 'Paracinematic Lives' of *Gravity's Rainbow.*" *Modern Fiction Studies* 29 (Winter 1983): 655-70.

Grady, R. F. Review of *The Crying of Lot 49. Best Sellers* 26 (May 1966): 76.

Grant, J. K. " 'Convention' and 'Neurosis,' 'Communion' and 'Tragedy': Thomas Pynchon, Iris Murdoch, Alain Robbe-Grillet." Seminar, MLA Convention. New York, 28 December 1976.

Graves, Lila V. "Love and the Western World of Pynchon's *V.*" *South Atlantic Review* 47 (January 1982): 62-73.

Gray, Paul. "Openers." Review of *Slow Learner. Time,* 23 April 1984, 81.

Green, Martin. *"The Crying of Lot 49:* Pynchon's Heart of Darkness." *Pynchon Notes* 8 (February 1982): 30-38.

Green, Martin B. "Personal Relations and Public Themes." *Commonweal,* 11 May 1979, 266-67.

Greenberg, Alvin. "The Underground Woman: An Excursion into the V-ness of Thomas Pyncheon" [*sic*]. *Chelsea* 27 (1969): 58-65.

Greiner, Donald J. "Fiction as History, History as Fiction: The Reader and Thomas Pynchon's *V.*" *South Carolina Review* 10, no. 1 (November 1977): 4-18.

————. "Pynchon, Hawkes, and Updike: Readers and the Paradox of Accessibility." *South Carolina Review* 16, no. 1 (November 1983): 45-51.

Gros, Charles G. Review of *V. Best Sellers* 23 (1 April 1963): 12.

Guetti, James. *Word-Music: The Aesthetic Aspect of Narrative Fiction.* New Brunswick, New Jersey: Rutgers University Press, 1980. 93-107.

————. "Aggressive Reading: Detective Fiction and Realistic Narrative." *Raritan* 2, no. 1 (1982): 133-54.

Gunton, Sharon R., ed. *Contemporary Literary Criticism: Excerpts from Criticism of the Works of Today's Novelists, Poets, Playwrights, and Other Creative Writers.* Detroit: Gale Research, 1981. 18:429-41.

Guzlowski, John Z. "No More Sea Changes: Hawkes, Pynchon, Gaddis, and Barth." *Critique* 23, no. 2 (Winter 1981-82): 48-60.

———. *"The Crying of Lot 49* and 'The Shadow.' " *Pynchon Notes* 9 (June 1982): 61-68.

———. Review of Schaub (1981). *Modern Fiction Studies* 28 (Summer 1982): 310-11.

———. "Masks and Maskings in Hawkes, Barth, Gaddis and Pynchon." *Journal of Evolutionary Psychology* 4, no. 3 (August 1983): 215-27.

———. "Hollow Gestures and Empty Words: Inconsequential Action and Dialogue in Recent American Novels." *Markham Review* 12, no. 2 (Winter 1983): 21-26.

Hall, James. "The New Pleasures of the Imagination." *Virginia Quarterly Review* 46 (Autumn 1970): 596-612.

Handlin, Oscar. Review of *The Crying of Lot 49. Atlantic Monthly,* May 1966, 127-28.

Harder, Kelsie B. "Names in Thomas Pynchon's *V." Literary Onomastics Studies* 5 (1978): 64-80.

Harmon, William. " 'Anti-Fiction' in American Humor." In *The Comic Imagination in American Literature,* edited by Louis D. Rubin. New Brunswick: Rutgers University Press, 1973. 373-83.

———. Review of Schaub (1981). *Southern Humanities Review* 17 (1983): 379-81.

Harrington, John P. "Pynchon, Beckett, and Entropy: Uses of Metaphor." *Missouri Review* 5, no. 3 (Summer 1982): 129-38.

Harris, Charles B. "Death and Absurdity: Thomas Pynchon and the Entropic Vision." In *Contemporary American Novelists of the Absurd.* New Haven: Yale College and University Press, 1971. 76-99.

Harris, Robert R. "A Talk with Don DeLillo." *New York Times Book Review,* 10 October 1982, 26.

Hartman, Carl. "The Fellowship of the Roles." Review of *V. Contact* 4 (July 1963): 73-75.

Hartman, Geoffrey H. "Literature High and Low: The Case of the Mystery Story." In *The Facts of Reading and Other Essays*. Chicago: University of Chicago Press, 1975. 203-22.

Hartnett, Michael. "Thomas Pynchon's Long Island Years." *Confrontation* 30/31 (November 1985): 44-48.

Hassan, Ihab. "The Futility Corner." Review of *V. Saturday Review,* 23 March 1963, 44.

———. *Contemporary American Literature, 1945-1972: An Introduction.* New York: Ungar, 1973. 56, 81, 84-85, 171.

Hathaway, Baxter. "Hathaway Recalls Cornell Writers of the 50's." *Cornell Daily Sun,* 5 May 1978, 31, 38.

Hauck, Richard Boyd. *A Cheerful Nihilism: Confidence and "The Absurd" in American Humorous Fiction.* Bloomington, Indiana: Indiana University Press, 1971. 11, 237, 242-43.

Hausdorff, Don. "Thomas Pynchon's Multiple Absurdities." *Wisconsin Studies in Contemporary Literature* 7 (Autumn 1966): 258-69.

Hayles, Katherine. "Cosmology and the Point of (No) Return in *Gravity's Rainbow.*" *Markham Review* 12, no. 4 (Summer 1983): 73-77.

———. *The Cosmic Web: Scientific Field Models and Literary Strategies in the 20th Century.* Ithaca: Cornell University Press, 1984. 168-97.

——— and Mary B. Eiser. "Coloring *Gravity's Rainbow.*" *Pynchon Notes* 16 (1985): 3-24.

Hays, Peter L. "Pynchon's 'Entropy': A Russian Connection." *Pynchon Notes* 16 (1985): 78-82.

———. "Pynchon's Cunning Lingual Novel: Communication in *Lot 49.*" *University of Mississippi Studies in English* 5 (1984-87): 23-38.

——— and Robert Redfield. "Pynchon's Spanish Source for 'Entropy.' " *Studies in Short Fiction* 16 (Fall 1979): 327-34.

Held, George. "Men on the Moon: American Novelists Explore Lunar Space." *Michigan Quarterly Review* 18 (1979): 318-42.

Hellman, Lillian. Individual comments in "Writer's Writers." *New York Times Book Review,* 4 December 1977, 3, 58.

Helterman, Jeffrey. *Thomas Pynchon's "Gravity's Rainbow": A Critical Commentary.* New York: Monarch Press, 1976.

Henderson, Harry B., III. *Versions of the Past: The Historical Imagination in American Fiction.* New York: Oxford University Press, 1974. 277-85.

Hendin, Josephine. "What Is Thomas Pynchon Telling Us?" *Harper's,* March 1975, 82, 85, 87-88, 90, 92. Reprinted in Pearce (1981), 42-50, and in Bloom (1986a), 37-46. Expanded as "Thomas Pynchon and Western Man" in Hendin's *Vulnerable People: A View of American Fiction Since 1945.* New York: Oxford University Press, 1978. 192-209.

———. "Experimental Fiction." In *Harvard Guide to Contemporary American Writing,* edited by Daniel Hoffman. Cambridge: Harvard University Press, 1979. 240-86 (281-86).

Henkle, Roger B. "Pynchon's Tapestries on the Western Wall." *Modern Fiction Studies* 17 (Summer 1971): 207-20. Reprinted in Mendelson (1978), 97-111.

———. "Pynchon in *Gravity's Rainbow:* Love Among the Runes, Or, Miltonic in the Gloaming." American Literature Seminar 268, MLA Convention. San Francisco, 28 December 1975.

———. Review of Plater (1978) and Siegel (1978). *Modern Fiction Studies* 25 (Summer 1979): 340-42.

———. "The Morning and the Evening Funnies: Comedy in *Gravity's Rainbow.*" In Clerc (1983), 273-90.

Hertzberg, Hendrick, and David C.K. McClelland. "Paranoia." *Harper's,* June 1974, 51-54, 59-60.

Herzberg, Bruce. "Selected Articles on Thomas Pynchon: An Annotated Bibliography." *Twentieth Century Literature* 21 (May 1975): 221-25. Reprinted as "Bibliography" in Levine and Leverenz (1976), 265-69.

———. "Breakfast, Death, Feedback: Thomas Pynchon and the Technologies of Interpretation." *Bucknell Review* 27, no. 2 (1983): 81-95.

Hicks, Granville. "A Plot Against the Post Office." Review of *The Crying of Lot 49. Saturday Review,* 30 April 1966, 27-28.

———. "The Prizes Authors Seek." *Publishers Weekly,* 20 May 1967, 35-36.

Hills, Rust. Review of *Gravity's Rainbow. Esquire,* September 1973, 10, 28.

Hipkiss, Robert A. "The Transcendental Quest Through Three Novels." Chap. 1 of *The American Absurd: Pynchon, Vonnegut, and Barth.* Port Washington, New York: Associated Faculty Press, 1984. 9-40.

Hirose, Eiichi. "1960-nendai amerika shosetsu to Pynchon" [Pynchon and the American Novel in the 1960s]. Afterword to *V.* (D1g), 2:317-35.

Hitchens, Christopher. "American Notes." *Times Literary Supplement,* 12 July 1985, 772.

Hite, Molly. "Holy-Center-Approaching in the Novels of Thomas Pynchon." *Journal of Narrative Technique* 12, no. 2 (Spring 1982): 121-29.

———. *Ideas of Order in the Novels of Thomas Pynchon.* Columbus, Ohio: Ohio State University Press, 1983.

———. "Influences, Parallels, Filiations." Review of Werner's *Paradoxical Resolutions. Pynchon Notes* 11 (February 1983): 57-62.

———. "Pynchon's Center of Gravity." *Markham Review* 12, no. 4 (Summer 1983): 71-73.

———. Review of Cooper (1983). *Sub-Stance* 44/45 (1985): 32-34.

———. Review of Clerc (1983). *Studies in American Fiction* 13 (1985): 111-12.

———. "Pynchon, Thomas, 1937- ." In *Contemporary Authors: A Bio-Bibliographical Guide to Current Writers,* edited by Deborah A. Straub. New Revision Series. Detroit: Gale Research Company, 1988. 22: 374-78.

Hoffman, Frederick J. "The Questing Comedian: Thomas Pynchon's *V.*" *Critique* 6, no. 3 (Winter 1963-64): 174-77.

Hoffman, Gerhard. "The Foregrounded Situation: New Narrative Strategies in Postmodern American Fiction." In *The American Identity: Fusion and Fragmentation,* edited by Rob Kroes. Amsterdam: Amerika Instituut, Universiteit van Amsterdam, 1980. 289-344.

Höge, Helmut. "Hintergründe-Inland." *Die Tageszeitung* [Berlin], 12 July 1986, 11.

Hohmann, Charles. *Thomas Pynchon's "Gravity's Rainbow": A Study of Its Conceptual Structure and of Rilke's Influence.* New York: Peter Lang, 1986.

Holdsworth, Carole A. "Fateful Labyrinths: *La Vida es sueño* and *The Crying of Lot 49.*" *Comparatist* 7 (May 1983): 57-74.

Hollander, Charles. "Pynchon's Inferno." *Cornell Alumni News* 81, no. 4 (November 1978): 24-30.

Holmes, John R. " 'A Hand to Turn the Time': History as Film in *Gravity's Rainbow.*" *Cithara* 23, no. 1 (November 1983): 5-16.

Holsberry, Carmen W. "Faulkner, Fitzgerald and Pynchon: Modernism and Postmodernism in Secondary School." *English Journal* 70, no. 2 (February 1981): 25-30.

Homberger, Eric. "Civility at Bay." Review of Berthoff's *A Literature Without Qualities. Times Literary Supplement,* 30 May 1980, 622.

Horvath, Brooke. "Linguistic Distancing in *Gravity's Rainbow.*" *Pynchon Notes* 8 (February 1982): 5-22.

———. Review of Newman (1986). *Modern Fiction Studies* 33 (Summer 1987): 333-37.

Hudson, Christopher. "Grand Delusions." *New Society,* December 1973, 608.

Hume, Kathryn. *Pynchon's Mythography: An Approach to "Gravity's Rainbow."* Carbondale: Southern Illinois University Press, 1987.

———. "Interfaces, Transitions, and Moires." Review of Moore (1987).

Pynchon Notes 18-19 (Spring-Fall 1986): 116-17.

———. "Gravity's Rainbow: Science Fiction, Fantasy, and Mythology." In Intersections: Fantasy & Science Fiction, edited by George E. Slusser and Eric S. Rabkin. Carbondale: Southern Illinois University Press, 1987. 190-200.

———, and Thomas J. Knight. "Orpheus and the Orphic Voice in Gravity's Rainbow." Philological Quarterly 64 (Summer 1985): 299-315.

———. "Pynchon's Orchestration of Gravity's Rainbow." Journal of English and Germanic Philology 85 (1986): 366-85.

Hunt, John W. "Comic Escape and Anti-Vision: The Novels of Joseph Heller and Thomas Pynchon." In Adversity and Grace: Studies in Recent American Literature, edited by Nathan A. Scott, Jr. Chicago: University of Chicago Press, 1969: 87-112. Excerpted as "Comic Escape and Anti-Vision: V. and The Crying of Lot 49" in Pearce (1981), 32-41.

Hyman, Stanley Edgar. "The Goddess and the Schlemihl." Review of V. New Leader, 18 March 1963, 22-23. Reprinted in Contemporary Literature, edited by Richard Kostelanetz. New York: Avon Books, 1964; expanded ed. 1969. 506-10. Also reprinted in Hyman's Standards: A Chronicle of Books for Our Time. New York: Horizon Press, 1966. 138-42.

Ickstadt, Heinz. "Thomas Pynchon: The Crying of Lot 49." In Amerikanische Erzählliteratur 1950-1970, edited by Freider Busch and Renate Schmidt-von Bardelben. Kritische Information 28. Munich: Fink, 1975. 126-41. Reprinted in Ickstadt (1981), 104-27.

———, ed. Ordnung und Entropie: zum Romanwerk von Thomas Pynchon [Order and Entropy: On the Work of Thomas Pynchon]. Reinbek bei Hamburg: Rowohlt, 1981.

"In Transatlantic Sally, PW Readers Select Top 12 (and 17) Novels." Publishers Weekly, 20 January 1984, 30.

Ingraham, Catherine. Review of Schaub (1981). Modern Language Notes 96 (1981): 1254-57.

————. "A Practical Duplicity." Review of Cooper (1983). *Pynchon Notes* 12 (June 1983): 52-55.

Isaacs, Neil D. "Thomas Pynchon: Old Myths, New Frontiers." In *Essays on the Contemporary American Novel,* edited by Hedwig Bock and Albert Wertheim. Munich: Max Hueber, 1986. 183-203.

Isernhagen, Hartwig. "Modernism/Postmodernism: Continuities of a 'Split' Repertoire of Narrative Themes and Strategies (A Provisional Restatement of a Traditional View of Twentieth Century Literary Avant-gardism)." In *Critical Angles: European Views of Contemporary American Literature,* edited by Marc Chénetier. Carbondale: Southern Illinois University Press, 1986. 15-28.

Isle, Walter. "The Large Loose Baggy Monsters of William Gaddis and Thomas Pynchon." American Literature Special Session 388, MLA Convention. New York, 28 December 1975.

Jackson, Rosemary. "From Kafka's 'Metamorphosis' to Pynchon's 'Entropy.' " Chap. 7 of *Fantasy: The Literature of Subversion.* New York: Methuen, 1981. 157-70.

Jardine, Alice A. *Gynesis: Configurations of Woman and Modernity.* Ithaca: Cornell University Press, 1986. 247-52.

Jayne, Edward. "The Dialectics of Paranoid Form." *Genre* 11, no. 1 (Spring 1978): 131-57.

Jelinek, Elfriede. "Kein Licht am Ende des Tunnels: Nachricten über Thomas Pynchon." *Manuskripte* 15, H52 (1976): 36-44.

————. "Nachwort." In *V.* (D1e), 530-49.

Jensen, Bo Green. " 'A Screaming comes across the sky. . . .' " *Vinduet* [Oslo, Norway] 40, no. 1 (1986): 10-17.

Johnston, John. "Postmodern Theory/Postmodern Fiction." *CLIO* 16, no. 2 (Winter 1987): 139-58.

Jones, Fiona K. "The Twentieth Century Writer and the Image of the Computer." In *Computers and Human Communication: Problems and Prospects,* edited by David L. Crowner and Laurence A. Marschall. Washington, D.C.: University Press of America, 1974. 167-80.

Jordan, Clive. "World Enough, and Time." *Encounter,* February 1974, 61-64.

Justus, James H. Review of Plater (1978). *American Literature* 51 (1980): 582-83.

Kadragic, Alma. "Robert Coover" [interview]. *Shantih* 2, no. 2 (1972): 57-60.

Kahn, Peter. Comments on Pynchon in "Remembering Nabokov: Cornell Colleagues and Others." In *The Achievements of Vladimir Nabokov: Essays, Studies, Reminiscences and Stories,* edited by George Gibian and Stephen Jan Parker. Ithaca: Cornell University Center for International Studies, 1984. 229-30.

Kappel, Lawrence. "Psychic Geography in *Gravity's Rainbow.*" *Contemporary Literature* 21 (Spring 1980): 225-51.

Karl, Frederick R. *American Fictions 1940-1980: A Comprehensive History and Critical Evaluation.* New York: Harper & Row, 1983. 302-11, 358-64, 444-47.

―――. "American Fictions: The Mega-Novel." *Conjunctions* 7 (1985): 248-60.

Kaufman, Marjorie. "Brünnhilde and the Chemists: Women in *Gravity's Rainbow.*" In Levine and Leverenz (1976), 197-227.

Kawin, Bruce F. *The Mind of the Novel: Reflexive Fiction and the Ineffable.* Princeton: Princeton University Press, 1982. 198-210, 345-46.

Kazin, Alfred. *The Bright Book of Life.* Boston: Little, Brown, 1973. 275-80.

―――. "American Writing Now." *New Republic,* 18 October 1980, 27-30.

Keesey, Douglas. "Nature and the Supernatural: Pynchon's Ecological Ghost Stories." *Pynchon Notes* 18-19 (Spring-Fall 1986): 84-95.

Kehl, D.G. "The Lost Word: Decadence in the Fiction of Thomas Pynchon." *Christianity Today,* 6 August 1976, 18, 20.

Kemp, Peter. "Pynchon." Review of Schaub (1981). *Times Literary Supplement,* 26 February 1982, 220.

———. "Literature as Micro-Dots." Review of Tanner (1982). *Listener,* 22 July 1982, 20.

Kerckhove, Derrick de. "Derrick de Kerckhove Replies to J.O. Tate." *Pynchon Notes* 15 (Fall 1984): 83.

Kermode, Frank. "The Use of the Codes." In *Approaches to Poetics,* edited by Seymour Chatman. New York: Columbia University Press, 1973. 68-74. Reprinted in Kermode's *The Art of Telling: Essays on Fiction.* Cambridge, Massachusetts: Harvard University Press, 1983. 72-91 (82-87). Reprinted as "Decoding the Trystero" in Mendelson (1978), 162-66, and as "The Use of Codes in *The Crying of Lot 49*" in Bloom (1986a), 11-14.

———. "Pynchon and the Modern Novel." *Granta,* 1976, 4-7.

———. "What Precisely Are the Facts?" in *The Genesis of Secrecy: On the Interpretation of Narrative.* Cambridge: Harvard University Press, 1979. 10-23.

Kettler, Robert. Review of *Gravity's Rainbow. Quartet* 7 (Winter 1974-75): 42-43.

Kharpertian, Theodore D. "Of Models, Muddles, and Middles: Menippean Satire and Pynchon's *V.*" *Pynchon Notes* 17 (Fall 1985): 3-14.

———. "On Origins and Beginnings." Review of Kim (1985). *Pynchon Notes* 18-19 (Spring-Fall 1986): 118-20.

Kiely, Robert. "Being Serious in the 'Sixties: Madness, Meaning, and Metaphor in *One Flew over the Cuckoo's Nest* and *The Crying of Lot 49.*" *Hebrew Studies in Literature and the Arts* 12 (1984): 215-37.

Kiernan, Robert F. *American Writing Since 1945: A Critical Survey.* New York: Unger, 1983. 59-60.

Kihss, Peter. "Pulitzer Jurors Dismayed on Pynchon." *New York Times,* 8 May 1974, 38.

Kim, Sang-Ku. "The World of Death in Thomas Pynchon's *V.*" *University Journal: Humanities* [Busan, Korea] 22 (1982): 141-60.

Kim, Seong-Kon. *Journey Into the Past: The Historical and Mythical Imagination of Barth and Pynchon.* Seoul: American Studies Institute, Seoul National University, 1985.

Kinsley, William. "Sexe et association dans *Tristram Shandy* et *Gravity's Rainbow.*" *Études françaises* 22, no. 1 (1986): 37-51.

Kirby, David K. "Two Modern Versions of the Quest." *Southern Humanities Review* 5 (Fall 1971): 387-95.

Klähn, Bernd. "Thomas Pynchon." In *Kritisches Lexicon zur fremdsprachigen Gegenwartsliteratur,* edited by Heinz Ludwig Arnold. Munich: Edition Text & Kritik, 1983. 1-10, A/1, B/1, D/1.

Klein, Marcus, ed. *The American Novel Since World War II.* Greenwich: Fawcett, 1969.

Klinkowitz, Jerome. "How Fiction Survives the Seventies." *North American Review* 258 (Fall 1973): 69-73.

———. *Literary Disruptions: The Making of Post-Contemporary American Fiction.* Urbana, Illinois: University of Illinois Press, 1975. 11-15.

———. Review of Plater (1978). *Journal of English and Germanic Philology* 78 (July 1979): 466-68.

———. Review of Stark (1980). *American Literature* 53 (May 1981): 335-36.

Kobayashi, Kenji. "Posuto-modanizumu kara kindai no chōkoku e-Thomas Pynchon soshite Toni Morrison." *Eigo Seinen* 132 (1986): 418-22.

Koch, Stephen. "Imagination in the Abstract." Review of *V. Antioch Review* 24 (Summer 1964): 253-63.

Kolodny, Annette, and Daniel James Peters. "Pynchon's *The Crying of Lot 49:* The Novel as Subversive Experience." *Modern Fiction Studies* 19 (Spring 1973): 79-87.

87

Kopcewicz, Andrzej. "The Rocket and the Whale: Thomas Pynchon's *Gravity's Rainbow* and *Moby Dick.*" In *Proceedings of a Symposium on American Literature,* edited by Marta Sienicka. Poznań: Adam Mickiewicz University Press, 1979. 145-50.

——. "Elements of Puritanism in Thomas Pynchon's *Gravity's Rainbow.*" In *Traditions in Twentieth Century American Literature.* Poznań: Adam Mickiewicz University Press, 1981. 133-45.

Kort, Wesley A. "The Possible Plots of Thomas Pynchon's Fiction." In *Moral Fiber: Character and Belief in Recent American Fiction.* Philadelphia: Fortress Press, 1982. 123-33.

Kostelanetz, Richard. "Notes on the American Short Story Today." *Minnesota Review* 5 (1965): 214-21.

——. "The Point Is That Life Doesn't Have Any Point." *New York Times Book Review,* 6 June 1965, 3, 28, 30.

——. "The Short Story in Search of Status." *Twentieth Century* 174, no. 1027 (Autumn 1965): 65-69.

——. "New American Fiction Reconsidered." *TriQuarterly* 8 (1967): 279-86.

——. "American Fiction of the Sixties." In *On Contemporary Literature,* edited by Kostelanetz. Expanded edition. New York: Avon Discus Books, 1969. 634-52.

——. "Dada and the Future Fiction." *Works* 1, no. 3 (1969): 58-66.

——. *The End of Intelligent Writing: Literary Politics in America.* New York: Sheed and Ward, 1974. 168, 324, 326-27, 338, 344-45.

——, ed. *The New American Arts.* New York: Horizon Press, 1965. 16, 22, 202-3, 214-17.

Kowalewski, Michael. "For Once, Then, Pynchon." *Texas Studies in Literature and Language* 28, no. 2 (Summer 1986): 182-208.

Krafft, John M. "Anarcho-Romanticism and the Metaphysics of Counter-force: Alex Comfort and Thomas Pynchon." *Paunch* 40-41 (April 1975): 78-107.

————. "And How Far-Fallen: Puritan Themes in *Gravity's Rainbow.*" *Critique* 18, no. 3 (1977): 55-73.

————. "Historical Imagination in the Novels of Thomas Pynchon." American Literature Session 703, MLA Convention. Chicago, 30 December 1977.

————. "Hit and Miss." Reviews of Cowart (1980) and Stark (1980). *Pynchon Notes* 4 (October 1980): 29-38.

————. "Thomas Pynchon." In *The 60's Without Apology,* edited by Sohnya Sayres, et al. Minneapolis: University of Minnesota Press, 1984. 108-12.

————. "Chelsea Morning." Review of Bloom (1986a and b). *Pynchon Notes* 18-19 (Spring-Fall 1986): 124-28.

Kramer, Victor A., and Dewey W. "German Madness as a Matrix for *Gravity's Rainbow:* Rilke, Mann and the Movement Away from the Spiritual." American Literature Session 703, MLA Convention. Chicago, 30 December 1977.

Kreutzer, Eberhard. *New York in der zeitgenoossischen amerikanischen Erzahlliteratur.* Heidelberg: Carl Winter, 1985. 147-51, 261-67, and passim.

Laird, D. Review of Newman (1986). *Choice* 24 (March 1987): 1062.

————. Review of Hume (1987). *Choice* 25 (December 1987): 622.

Lakoff, Robin. "Remarks on *This* and *That.*" In *Papers from the Tenth Regional Meeting/Chicago Linguistic Society,* edited by Michael W. La Galy, et al. Chicago: Chicago Linguistic Society, 1974. 345-56.

Langbaum, Robert. "The Long Life of Modernism." Review of McConnell's *Four Postwar American Novelists. Partisan Review* 48 (1981): 151-60.

Langland, Elizabeth. "Pynchon's Everyman: Searching for an Alternative Society in *The Crying of Lot 49.*" In *Society in the Novel.* Chapel Hill: University of North Carolina Press, 1984. 202-8.

Larner, Jeremy. "The New Schlemihl." Review of *V. Partisan Review* 30 (Summer 1963): 273-76.

Larsson, Donald. "From A to *V.:* The Paranoid Symbol in American Literature." Paper presented at the American Culture Association/ Popular Culture Association Conference, April 1979.

——. "The Camera Eye: 'Cinematic' Narrative in *U.S.A.* and *Gravity's Rainbow.*" In *Ideas of Order in Literature and Film,* edited by Peter Ruppert. Tallahassee: University Presses of Florida, 1980. 94-106.

——. "Approach and Avoid: Douglas A. Mackey's *The Rainbow Quest* of Thomas Pynchon." *Pynchon Notes* 7 (October 1981): 49, 52.

——. Entry on Pynchon in *Critical Survey of Short Fiction,* edited by Frank N. Magill. Englewood Cliffs, New Jersey: Salem Press, 1981. 6:2141-47.

——. "The Secret Integration." In *Masterplots II: Short Story Series,* edited by Frank N. Magill. Englewood Cliffs, New Jersey: Salem Press, 1986. 5:2053-56.

——. "Under the Rose." In *Masterplots II: Short Story Series,* edited by Frank N. Magill. Englewood Cliffs, N.J.: Salem Press, 1986. 6:2464-67.

——. "Partially Understanding Pynchon." Review of Newman (1986). *Pynchon Notes* 18-19 (Spring-Fall 1986): 121-23.

LaSalle, Peter. " 'Sumer is icumen in Llude sing cuccu'!" Review of *Slow Learner. America,* 7-14 July 1984, 16-17.

Leary, Timothy. "Kekule's Dream Serpent Makes a Good Logo." *Spit in the Ocean* 3 (Fall 1977): 94-98.

——. *Flashbacks: An Autobiography.* Los Angeles: J. P. Tarcher, 1983. 346, 355-56, 361.

——. "Ecstatic Electricity." *NY Talk,* August 1985, 34.

——. "Cyberpunks." *Spin,* April 1987, 88, 90-93 (91-92).

LeClair, Thomas. "Death and Black Humor." *Critique* 17, no. 1 (1975): 5-40.

———. "An Ear to America." Review of Gaddis's *J R. Commonweal,* 16 January 1976, 54-55.

———. "Moral Criticism." Review of Gardner's *On Moral Fiction* and Hendin's *Vulnerable People. Contemporary Literature* 20 (1979): 508-12.

———. "Missing Writers." *Horizon,* October 1981, 48-52.

———. "William Gaddis, *J R,* & The Art of Excess." *Modern Fiction Studies* 27 (1981): 587-600.

———. Review of Clerc (1983). *American Literature* 55 (1983): 485-86.

———. "Postmodern Mastery." In *Postmodern Fiction: A Bio-Bibliographical Guide,* edited by Larry McCaffery. New York: Greenwood Press, 1986. 117-28.

———. *In the Loop: Don DeLillo and the Systems Novel.* Urbana: University of Illinois Press, 1987. 13, 19, 61, and passim.

———. "Prologue: Thomas Pynchon's *Gravity's Rainbow.*" In *The Art of Excess.* Urbana: University of Illinois Press, 1989.

———, and Larry McCaffery, eds. *Anything Can Happen: Interviews with Contemporary American Novelists.* Urbana: University of Illinois Press, 1983.

Lehan, Richard. "The American Novel—A Survey of 1966." *Wisconsin Studies in Contemporary Literature* 8 (Summer 1967): 437-49.

———. *A Dangerous Crossing.* Carbondale: Southern Illinois University Press, 1973. 157-62.

Lehmann-Haupt, Christopher. "End-of-the-World Machine." Review of *The Crying of Lot 49. New York Times,* 3 June 1966, 37.

———. "The Adventures of Rocketman." Review of *Gravity's Rainbow. New York Times,* 9 March 1973, 35.

———. "The Limits of a Novel's Point of View." *New York Times,* 19 January 1984, C18.

———. Review of *Slow Learner. New York Times,* 29 March 1984, C24.

Leland, John P. "Pynchon's Linguistic Demon: *The Crying of Lot 49.*" *Critique* 16, no. 2 (1974): 45-53.

Lense, Edward. "Pynchon's *V.*" *Explicator* 43 (Fall 1984): 60-61.

Leonard, John. "The Third Law of Reviewer Emotion." *New York Times Book Review,* 10 June 1973, 47.

―――. "1973: An Apology and 38 Consolations." *New York Times Book Review,* 2 December 1973, 1.

―――. "Pulitzer People Are No Prize." *New York Times Book Review,* 19 May 1974, 47.

Leverenz, David. "Point Counterpoint." *Partisan Review* 42 (1975): 643-44.

―――. "On Trying to Read *Gravity's Rainbow.*" In Levine and Leverenz (1976), 229-49.

Levine, Al. "Paranoia of the Most Grandiose Proportions." Review of *Gravity's Rainbow. Commonweal,* 4 May 1973, 217-18.

Levine, George. "V-2." *Partisan Review* 40 (Fall 1973): 517-29. Reprinted in Mendelson (1978), 178-91.

―――. "Politics and the Form of Disenchantment." *College English* 36 (December 1974): 422-35.

―――. "Risking the Moment: Anarchy and Possibility in Pynchon's Fiction." In Levine and Leverenz (1976), 113-36. Reprinted as "Risking the Moment" in Bloom (1986a), 59-77.

―――, and David Leverenz, eds. *Mindful Pleasures: Essays on Thomas Pynchon.* Boston: Little, Brown, 1976.

Levine, Paul. "Easterns and Westerns." Review of *V. Hudson Review* 16 (Autumn 1963): 455-62.

Levitt, Morton P. "Honored Past? Fearsome Present?: Pynchon, Coover, Doctorow, and Barth and the American Rendering of Myth." In *Modernist Survivors: The Contemporary Novel in England, the United States, France, and Latin America.* Columbus: Ohio State University Press, 1987. 73-123 (76-91).

LeVot, André. "The Rocket and the Pig: Thomas Pynchon and Science Fiction." *Caliban* 12, no. 2 (1975): 111-18.

————. "Disjunctive and Conjunctive Modes in Contemporary American Fiction." *Forum* 14, no. 1 (1976): 44-55 (52-53).

————. "Contre l'entropie: les stratègies de la fiction amèricaine postmoderniste." *Recherches anglaises et amèricaines* 10 (1977): 298-319.

Lewicki, Zbigniew. "Thomas Pynchon, or, The Inevitability of Destruction." In *The Bang and the Whimper: Apocalypse and Entropy in American Literature.* Westport, Connecticut: Greenwood, 1984. 85-101.

Lewis, R. W. B. *Trials of the Word: Essays in American Literature and the Humanistic Tradition.* New Haven: Yale University Press, 1965. 228-34.

Lewis, Roger. "Drawn From Life." Review of *Slow Learner. New Statesman,* 11 January 1985, 34.

Lhamon, W. T., Jr. "The Most Irresponsible Bastard." Review of *Gravity's Rainbow. New Republic,* 14 April 1973, 24-28.

————. "Pentecost, Promiscuity and Pynchon's *V.:* From the Scaffold to the Impulsive." *Twentieth Century Literature* 21 (May 1975): 163-76. Reprinted in Levine and Leverenz (1976), 69-86.

————. "Pynchon's Dodgy Politics." American Literature Special Session 388, MLA Convention. New York, 28 December 1976.

Limon, John Keith. "How to Place Poe's Arthur Gordon Pym in Science-Dominated Intellectual History, and How to Extract It Again." *North Dakota Quarterly* 51, no. 1 (1983): 31-47.

Lindroth, James R. Review of *The Crying of Lot 49. America* 114, no. 20 (14 May 1966): 700.

————. "A Bonus for Fiction Buffs." Review of *Gravity's Rainbow. America* 128, no. 18 (12 May 1973): 446.

Lippman, Bertram. "The Reader of Movies: Thomas Pynchon's *Gravity's Rainbow." Denver Quarterly* 12, no. 1 (1977): 1-46.

Lipsius, Frank. "The American Lit Fit." Review of *Gravity's Rainbow*. *Books and Bookmen,* March 1974, 64-66.

Lish, Gordon. "For Jeromé—with Love and Kisses." In *What I Know So Far*. New York: Holt, Rinehart and Winston, 1984. 105-63 (151-53).

Locke, Richard. "One of the longest, most difficult, most ambitious American novels in years." Review of *Gravity's Rainbow*. *New York Times Book Review,* 11 March 1973, 1-3, 12, 14.

―――. "The Literary View: What I Like." *New York Times Book Review,* 15 May 1977, 3, 36-37.

Loofbourow, John W. "Realism in the Anglo-American Novel: The Pastoral Myth." In *The Theory of the Novel: New Essays,* edited by John Halperin. New York: Oxford University Press, 1974. 257-70 (267-70).

Lundkvist, Artur. "Mardrömmar och spex." *Bonniers litterära magasin* 42, no. 5 (1973): 276-81.

―――. "Thomas Pynchon." In *Fantasi med realism om nutida utländsk skönlitteratur*. Stockholm: Liber Förlag, 1979. 173-80.

Lyons, Thomas R., and Allan D. Franklin. "Thomas Pynchon's 'Classic' Presentation of the Second Law of Thermodynamics." *Bulletin of the Rocky Mountain Modern Language Association* 27 (1973): 195-204.

MacAdam, Alfred. "Pynchon as Satirist: To Write, To Mean." *Yale Review* 67 (Summer 1978): 555-66.

Macdonald, Gina. Biographical sketch in *Twentieth-Century Science-Fiction Writers,* 2d ed., edited by Curtis C. Smith. London: St. James Press, 1986. 587-89.

Mackey, Douglas A. *The Rainbow Quest of Thomas Pynchon*. San Bernardino, California: Borgo Press, 1980.

Mackey, Louis. "Paranoia, Pynchon, and Preterition." *Sub-Stance* 30 (1981): 16-30. Reprinted in Bloom (1986b), 53-67.

———. "Thomas Pynchon and the American Dream." *Pynchon Notes* 14 (February 1984): 7-22.

Maddocks, Melvin. "Paleface Takeover." Review of *Gravity's Rainbow. Atlantic Monthly,* March 1973, 98-101.

Mahon, Derek. Individual comments on *The Crying of Lot 49* in "The Pleasures of Reading: 1984." *New Statesman,* 21-28 December 1984, 44.

Malkin, Mary Ann. Review of *The Crying of Lot 49. Antiquarian Bookman* 37 (16 May 1966): 2134.

Mangel, Anne. "Maxwell's Demon, Entropy, Information: *The Crying of Lot 49.*" *TriQuarterly* 20 (Winter 1971): 194-208. Reprinted in Levine and Leverenz (1976), 87-100. Translated into Polish by Piotr Siemion as "Demon Maxwella, Entropia, Informacja: *49 idzie pod mlotek,*" *Literatura na Świecie* 7/168 (1985): 210-24.

Mansur, Carole. Review of *Slow Learner. Punch,* 30 January 1985, 53.

"A Marathon on Pynchon Stirs Readers." *New York Times,* 15 November 1987, 61.

Marcus, Steven. "Reading the Illegible: Modern Representations of Urban Experience." *Southern Review* 22 (1986): 443-64 (459-64). Modified version reprinted in *Visions of the Modern City: Essays in History, Art, and Literature,* edited by William Sharpe and Leonard Wallock. New York: Columbia University Press, 1983. 228-43 (241-43).

Marowski, Daniel G., and Jean C. Stine, eds. *Contemporary Literary Criticism: Excerpts from Criticism of the Works of Today's Novelists, Poets, Playwrights, Short Story Writers, Scriptwriters, and Other Creative Writers.* Detroit: Gale Research, 1985. 33:327-40.

Marquez, Antonio. Review of Siegel (1978). *Rocky Mountain Review of Language and Literature* 33, no. 2 (1979): 82.

———. "The Cinematic Imagination in Thomas Pynchon's *Gravity's Rainbow.*" *Rocky Mountain Review of Language and Literature* 33, no. 4 (Fall 1979): 165-79.

———. "Technologique in *Gravity's Rainbow.*" *Research Studies* 48, no. 1 (March 1980): 1-10.

──────. "The Nightmare of History and Thomas Pynchon's *Gravity's Rainbow.*" *Essays in Literature* 8, no. 1 (Spring 1981): 53-62.

──────. "Everything Is Connected: Paranoia in *Gravity's Rainbow.*" *Perspectives on Contemporary Literature* 9 (1983): 92-104.

Marriott, David. "*Gravity's Rainbow:* Apocryphal History or Historical Apocrypha?" *Journal of American Studies* 19, no. 1 (April 1985): 69-80.

──────. "Moviegoing." *Pynchon Notes* 16 (1985): 46-77.

Martin, Richard. "Clio Bemused: The Uses of History in Contemporary American Fiction." *Sub-Stance* 27 (1980): 13-24.

Mateo, Leopoldo. "La vision apocaliptica de Thomas Pynchon." In *Actas del primer congreso de la asociación española de estudios anglo-americanos: Granada 15 al 17 de diciembre 1977.* Granada: Universidad de Granada, 1978. 49-52.

Materer, Timothy. *Wyndham Lewis the Novelist.* Detroit: Wayne State University Press, 1976. 165.

Mathieson, Kenneth. "The Influence of Science Fiction in the Contemporary American Novel." *Science-Fiction Studies* 12, no. 1 (1985): 22-32 (30-31).

Matthijs, Michel. "Character in Pynchon's *V.*" *Restant* 10, no. 2 (Summer 1982): 125-44.

May, John R. *Toward a New Earth: Apocalypse in the American Novel.* Notre Dame, Indiana: University of Notre Dame Press, 1972. 180-91.

Mayberry, George and Sharon. Review of *The Crying of Lot 49. Nation,* 5 February 1973, 182.

Mazurek, Raymond A. "Ideology and Form in the Postmodernist Historical Novel: *The Sot-Weed Factor* and *Gravity's Rainbow.*" *Minnesota Review* n.s. 25 (1985): 69-84.

McCaffery, Larry, and Sinda Gregory, eds. *Alive and Writing: Interviews with American Authors of the 1980s.* Urbana: University of Illinois Press, 1987.

McCarron, William E. "Coincidental and Contrived Dates in *Gravity's Rainbow.*" *Pynchon Notes* 17 (Fall 1985): 84-85.

———. "Pynchon and Hogarth." *Notes on Contemporary Literature* 16, no. 5 (November 1986): 2.

———. "Pynchon and Hobbes." *Notes on Contemporary Literature* 17, no. 1 (January 1987): 12.

McClintock, James I. "United State Revisited: Pynchon and Zamiatin." *Contemporary Literature* 18 (Autumn 1977): 475-90.

McConnell, Frank D. "Thomas Pynchon." In *Contemporary Novelists of the English Language,* edited by James Vinson. New York: St. Martin's Press, 1972. 1033-36. Revised and expanded text in 3rd edition (1982), 542-43.

———. "The Corpse of the Dragon: Notes on Post-romantic Fiction." *TriQuarterly* 33 (Spring 1975): 273-303.

———. "Thomas Pynchon and the Abreaction of the Lord of Night." Chap. 4 of *Four Postwar American Novelists: Bellow, Mailer, Barth and Pynchon.* Chicago: University of Chicago Press, 1977. 159-97.

———. "Stalking Papa's Ghost: Hemingway's Presence in Contemporary American Writing." In *Ernest Hemingway: New Critical Essays,* edited by A. Robert Lee. Totowa, New Jersey: Barnes & Noble, 1983. 193-211.

McDonough, Tom. "That Great Blank Page, the Screen." *New York Times Book Review,* 15 November 1987, 1, 41-43.

McDowell, Edwin. "Gobbledygook and Mangled Syntax." *New York Times Book Review,* 25 April 1982, 24.

———. "5 Pynchon Stories To Be Published in '84." *New York Times,* 23 September 1983, C20.

———. "Publishing: Pulitzer Controversies." *New York Times,* 11 May 1984, C26.

McElroy, Joseph. "Neural Neighborhoods and Other Concrete Abstracts." *TriQuarterly* 34 (Fall 1975): 210-17 (215-17).

McHale, Brian. "Modernist Reading, Post-Modern Text: The Case of *Gravity's Rainbow.*" *Poetics Today* 1, no. 1-2 (1979): 85-110. Reprinted in *Der amerikanische Roman nach 1945.* Darmstadt: Wissenschaftliche Buchgesellschaft, 1987. 415-46.

———. Review of Fowler (1980). *Sub-Stance* 30 (1981): 99-102.

———. "On Moral Fiction: One Use of *Gravity's Rainbow.*" *Pynchon Notes* 6 (June 1981): 34-38.

———. "Thomas Pynchon: A Portrait of the Artist as a Missing Person." *Cencrastus,* no. 5 (1981): 2-3. Translated into Hebrew by Gideon Roury as "Thomas Pynchon: Diyoknoh Shel na-Oman ke-Ne'edar." *Siman Kri' a* 14 (1981): 143-45.

———. "Unmaking the Well-Made Short Story/Making Up the Novel." *American Book Review* 8, no. 1 (November-December 1985): 16-18.

———. " 'You Used to Know What These Words Mean': Misreading *Gravity's Rainbow.*" *Language and Style* 18, no. 1 (1985): 93-118.

———. "Change of Dominant from Modernist to Postmodernist Writing." In *Approaching Postmodernism,* edited by Douwe Fokkema and Hans Bertens. Amsterdam: John Benjamins, 1986. 53-79.

———. *Postmodernist Fiction.* New York: Methuen, 1987. 21-25, and passim.

McHoul, Alec. "Labyrinths: Writing Radical Hermeneutics and the Post-ethical." *Philosophy Today* 31 (Fall 1987): 211-22.

———. "Telegrammatology Part I: *Lot 49* and the Post-ethical." *Pynchon Notes* 18-19 (Spring-Fall 1986): 39-54.

McLellan, Joseph. "Thomas Pynchon: A Short Mystery." *Washington Post Bookworld,* 11 March 1973, 2.

———. "Paperbacks." *Washington Post Bookworld,* 7 April 1974, 4.

McNamara, Eugene. "The Absurd Style in Contemporary American Literature." *Humanities Association Bulletin* 19, no. 1 (1968): 44-49.

McNeil, Helen. "Romance, Research, Melodrama: American Literature." *Encounter,* July 1979, 72-77.

Meikle, Jeffrey L. " 'Other Frequencies': The Parallel Worlds of Thomas Pynchon and H.P. Lovecraft." *Modern Fiction Studies* 27 (Summer 1981): 287-94.

———. "The Culture of Plasticity: Observations on Contemporary Cultural Transformation." *Amerikastudien* 28 (1983): 205-18.

Meixner, John A. "The All-Purpose Quest." Review of *V. Kenyon Review* 25 (Autumn 1963): 729-35.

Meltzer, Richard. "This Book Stinks." In *Essaying Essays: Alternative Forms of Exposition,* edited by Richard Kostelanetz. New York: Out of London Press, 1975. 196.

Mendelson, Edward. "Pynchon's Gravity." *Yale Review* 62 (Summer 1973): 624-31. Reprinted in Bloom (1986a), 15-21.

———. "Rainbow Corner." Review of Slade (1974). *Times Literary Supplement,* 13 June 1975, 666.

———. "The Sacred, The Profane, and *The Crying of Lot 49.*" In *Individual and Community: Variations on a Theme in American Fiction,* edited by Kenneth Baldwin and David Kirby. Durham, North Carolina: Duke University Press, 1976: 182-222. Reprinted (revised and abridged) in Mendelson (1978), 112-46.

———. "Gravity's Encyclopedia." In Levine and Leverenz (1976), 161-96. Reprinted in Bloom (1986b), 29-52.

———. "Encyclopedic Narrative: From Dante to Pynchon." *Modern Language Notes* 91 (December 1976): 1267-75.

———. "Schaub's Pynchon." Review of Schaub (1981). *Pynchon Notes* 7 (October 1981): 43-48.

———. Letter to the editors. *Pynchon Notes* 12 (June 1983): 56-57.

———. "How Gravity Began." Review of Pynchon's *Slow Learner. New Republic,* 16-23 July 1984, 36-39.

———, ed. *Pynchon: A Collection of Critical Essays.* Englewood Cliffs, N.J.: Prentice Hall, 1978.

Merrill, Dotson. "Pynchon's *V.:* 'The master is gone, the crew is gone, I am

here and I am painting the ship.' " Paper presented at the Rocky
Mountain Modern Language Association's Pynchon seminar, October
1978.

Merrill, Robert. "The Form and Meaning of Pynchon's *The Crying of Lot
49.*" *Ariel: A Review of International English Literature* 8, no. 1
(1977): 53-71.

————. Review of Moore (1987). *American Literature* 60 (March 1988):
136-37.

Mesher, David R. "Corrigenda: A Note on *Gravity's Rainbow.*" *Pynchon
Notes* 5 (February 1981): 13-16.

————. "Negative Entropy and the Form of *Gravity's Rainbow.*" *Research
Studies* 49, no. 3 (September 1981): 162-70.

————. "Pynchon and Nabokov's *V.*" *Pynchon Notes* 8 (February 1982):
43-46.

Mesic, Penelope. Review of Fowler (1980). *Booklist* 77 (15 December
1980): 554.

Michaelson, Robin. "Princeton Students Brave the Elements in 40-Hour
Read-athon of 800-page Novel." *Star Ledger* [Newark], 15 November
1987, 96.

Miers, Paul. Review of Hofstadter's *Gödel, Escher, Bach: An Eternal
Golden Braid. Modern Language Notes* 94 (1979): 1214-18.

Miller, James, Jr. *Quests Surd and Absurd: Essays in American Literature.* Chicago: University of Chicago Press, 1967. 15-16.

Mills, John. Review of *Gravity's Rainbow. Queen's Quarterly* 80 (Winter
1973): 648-49.

Mirkowicz, Tomasz. "Apokalipsa po amerykańsku." *Literatura na
Świecie* 7/168 (1985): 280-89.

Miyake, Takuo. "*V.* ni tsuitel." Afterword to *V.* (D1g), 2: 305-16.

————. "Pynchon *V.* no okeru 'Katari': sono tayosei no shikumi." In *Suga
yasuo, ogoshi kazugo: ryokyoju taikan kinen ronbundhu.* Kyoto:
Apollonsha, 1980. 953-65.

Miyamoto, Yoichiro. "Meikyu no naka no *V.*" [*V.* in the Labyrinth]. In *Bungaku to america: ohashi kenzaburo kyoju kanreki kinen ronbushu.* Tokyo: Nan'un-do, 1980. 1:239-53.

———. "Meta-fiction—The City in Barthelme and Pynchon." *Eigo Seinen: The Rising Generation* 129, no. 2 (1983): 66-67.

Mizener, Arthur. "Thomas Pynchon: 'Entropy.' " In *A Handbook of Analyses, Questions, and a Discussion of Technique for Use with "Modern Short Stories: The Uses of Imagination, Third Edition"* [B10i]. New York: Norton, 1971. 94-102.

———. "The New Romance." *Southern Review* 8 (Winter 1972): 106-17.

Moddelmog, Debra A. "The Oedipus Myth and Reader Response in Pynchon's *The Crying of Lot 49.*" *Papers on Language and Literature* 23 (Spring 1987): 240-49.

Molander, Roger. "How I Learned to Start Worrying and Hate the Bomb." *Washington Post,* 21 March 1982, D1, D5.

Monaghan, Charles. "Book Report: In the Margin." *Book World,* 12 April 1987, 15.

Monahan, Matthew. "Thomas Pynchon: A Bibliographical Checklist." *American Book Collector* n.s. 5, no. 3 (May/June 1984): 37-39.

Montrose, David. "Conventional Wisdom." Review of Tanner (1982). *New Statesman,* 28 May 1982, 20-21.

Mooney, Barbara. Letter to the editors. *Pynchon Notes* 12 (June 1983): 57.

Moore, Steven. "I Ching." *A Wake Newslitter: Studies of James Joyce's "Finnegans Wake"* 17 (1980): 25.

———. "Pynchon on Record." *Pynchon Notes* 10 (October 1982): 56-57.

———. " 'Parallel, Not Series': Thomas Pynchon and William Gaddis." *Pynchon Notes* 11 (February 1983): 6-26.

———. " 'The World Is at Fault.' " *Pynchon Notes* 15 (Fall 1984): 84-85.

———. Review of Moore (1987), Hume (1987), Hohmann (1986), Newman (1986), and Bloom (1986a and b). *Review of Contemporary*

Fiction 8, no. 2 (Summer 1988): 321-23.

———. Review of Seed (1988) and Weisenburger (1988). *Review of Contemporary Fiction* 8, no. 3 (Fall 1988): 174-75.

Moore, Thomas. "A Decade of *Gravity's Rainbow,* the Incredible Moving Film." *Michigan Quarterly Review* 22, no. 1 (Winter 1983): 78-94.

———. *The Style of Connectedness: "Gravity's Rainbow" and Thomas Pynchon.* Columbia: University of Missouri Press, 1987.

Morgan, Speer. "*Gravity's Rainbow:* What's the Big Idea?" *Modern Fiction Studies* 23 (Summer 1977): 119-216. Reprinted in Pearce (1981), 82-98.

Morris, Robert K. "Jumping Off the Golden Gate Bridge." Review of *Gravity's Rainbow. Nation,* 16 July 1973, 53-54.

Morrison, Philip. Review of *Gravity's Rainbow. Scientific American,* October 1973, 131. Reprinted in Mendelson (1978), 191-92.

Morse, J. Mitchell. Review of *The Crying of Lot 49. Hudson Review* 19 (Autumn 1966): 507-14.

Mottram, Eric. "Pynchon, Thomas." Entry in *Penguin Companion to American Literature,* edited by Malcolm Bradbury, Eric Mottram and Jean Franco. New York: McGraw-Hill, 1971. 211.

Mount, Ferdinand. "The Lonely American." Review of *Slow Learner. Spectator,* 26 January 1985, 23-24.

Moynahan, Julian. "Misguided Missiles." Review of *Gravity's Rainbow. Observer,* 18 November 1973, 39.

Muste, John. "Thomas Pynchon/Gwenhidwy: Who's Behind that Beard?" *Notes on Modern American Literature* 5, no. 2 (Spring 1981): item 13.

———. "The Mandala in *Gravity's Rainbow." Boundary 2* 9 (Winter 1981): 163-79.

———. "Singing Back the Silence: *Gravity's Rainbow* and the War Novel." *Modern Fiction Studies* 30 (Spring 1984): 5-23.

———. "*Gravity's Rainbow.*" In *Masterplots II: American Fiction Series,* edited by Frank N. Magill. Englewood Cliffs, New Jersey: Salem Press, 1986. 2:661-65.

"A Myth of Alligators." Review of *V. Time,* 15 March 1963, 106.

Nadeau, Robert L. "Readings from the New Book of Nature: Physics and Pynchon's *Gravity's Rainbow.*" *Studies in the Novel* 11 (Winter 1979): 454-71. Reprinted in *Readings from the New Book of Nature: Physics and Metaphysics in the Modern Novel.* Boston: University of Massachusetts Press, 1981.

Nakagawa, Yukiko. "T. Pynchon *V.* no kosei to style." In *Suga yasuo, ogoshi kazugo: royokoju taikan kinen ronbunshu.* Kyoto: Appollonsha, 1980. 940-52.

Nakamure, Eiichi. "Thomas Pynchon: kakusan to hokai." In *American bungaku no shintenkai: dai z-ji sekaitaisen go no shosetsu.* Kyoto: Yamaguchi, 1983. 506-30.

Nelson, Milton E., Jr. "A Thrust at Truth?" Review of *The Crying of Lot 49. Chicago Tribune Books Today,* 8 May 1966, 5.

Nelson, William. "The Humor and Humanizing of Outrage." *Thalia* 2, no. 1-2 (1979): 31-34.

New, Melvyn. "Profaned and Stenciled Texts: In Search of Pynchon's *V.*" *Georgia Review* 33 (Summer 1979): 395-412. Reprinted in Bloom (1986a), 93-109.

Newman, Robert D. "Pynchon's Use of Carob in *V.*" *Notes on Contemporary Literature* 11, no. 3 (May 1981): 11.

———. "The White Goddess Restored: Affirmation in Pynchon's *V.*" *University of Mississippi Studies in English* n.s. 4 (1983): 178-86.

———. *Understanding Thomas Pynchon.* Columbia: University of South Carolina Press, 1986.

Newport, John P. "Thomas Pynchon." In *Christianity and Contemporary Art Forms.* Waco, Texas: Word, 1979. 55-57.

"Newsmakers" [reprint of photo from *New York,* 13 May 1974]. *Newsweek,* 20 May 1974, 69.

Nichols, Lewis. "Author." *New York Times Book Review,* 28 April 1963, 8.

———. "Publisher's Row." *New York Times Book Review,* 2 January 1966, 8.

Nicholson, C. E., and R. W. Stevenson. *Thomas Pynchon: "The Crying of Lot 49."* York Note Series. New York: Longman, 1981.

———. " 'Words You Never Wanted to Hear': Fiction, History and Narratology in *The Crying of Lot 49.*" In *Tropic Crucible: Self and Theory in Language and Literature,* edited by Colin E. Nicholson and Ranjit Chatterjee. Singapore: Singapore University Press, 1984. 297-315. Reprinted in *Pynchon Notes* 16 (1985): 89-109.

Norhnberg, James. "Pynchon's Paraclete." In Mendelson (1978), 147-61.

Nokes, David. "Formal Complexities, Moral Preoccupations." Review of Tanner (1982). *Times Educational Supplement,* 9 July 1982, 21.

Nordell, Roderick. "Pynchon's Monstrous Parable/Parabola." Review of *Gravity's Rainbow. Christian Science Monitor,* 23 May 1973, 11.

"Nosepicking Contests." Review of *The Crying of Lot 49. Time,* 6 May 1966, 109.

Numasawa, Koji. "Black Humor: An American Aspect." *Studies in English Literature* [University of Tokyo] 44 (1968): 177-93.

O'Connell, Shaun. "Critical Condition." *Massachusetts Review* 22 (Spring 1981): 185-202.

O'Connor, Peter. "The Wasteland of Thomas Pynchon's *V.*" *College Literature* 3, no. 1 (Winter 1976): 49-55.

O'Donnell, Patrick. "Explaining Thomas Pynchon." Review of Plater (1978) and Levine and Leverenz (1976). *International Fiction Review* 6, no. 2 (1979): 152-56.

————. *"V."* In *Masterplots II: American Fiction Series,* edited by Frank N. Magill. Englewood Cliffs, New Jersey: Salem Press, 1986. 4:1727-32.

————. "A Book of Traces: *Gravity's Rainbow."* In *Passionate Doubts: Designs of Interpretation in Contemporary American Fiction.* Iowa City: University of Iowa Press, 1986. 73-94.

Olderman, Raymond Michael. "The Illusion and the Possibility of Conspiracy." In *Beyond the Wasteland: a Study of the American Novel in the 1960s.* New Haven: Yale University Press, 1972. 123-49.

————. "Freaks, Freak Humor, Thomas Pynchon's *Gravity's Rainbow* and the Freak Mythology." Paper presented at the MLA Convention's special session on Pynchon, December 1975.

————. "Thomas Pynchon." Review of Plater (1978) and Siegel (1978). *Contemporary Literature* 20 (Autumn 1979): 500-507.

————. "The New Consciousness and the Old System." In Clerc (1983), 199-228.

Oleksy, Elżbieta. "Perceval and Gawain: Ken Kesey's *One Flew over the Cuckoo's Nest* and Thomas Pynchon's *The Crying of Lot 49."* In *Proceedings of the Second April Conference of University Teachers of English,* edited by Irene Kałuża. Cracow: Uniwersytet Jagielloński, 1981. 167-77. Reprinted as "Kesey and Pynchon: A Trip to the Wasteland." *Revue belge de philologie et d'histoire* 64 (1986): 520-31.

Oleneva, Valentina I. *Modernitskaya novella SSHA 60-70-e gody* [The Modernist Short Story: The '60s and '70s]. Kiev: Naukova Dumka, 1985. 229-45.

Olsen, Lance. "Pynchon's New Nature: The Uncertainty Principle and Indeterminacy in *The Crying of Lot 49." Canadian Review of American Studies* 14, no. 2 (Summer 1983): 153-63. Revised and reprinted as "Pynchon's New Nature: Indeterminacy and *The Crying of Lot 49"* in *Ellipse of Uncertainty: An Introduction to Postmodern Fantasy.* New York: Greenwood, 1987. 69-83.

————. "Deconstructing the Enemy of Color: The Fantastic in *Gravity's Rainbow." Studies in the Novel* 18, no. 1 (Spring 1986): 74-86.

"175 High Spots/Some Leading Campaigns: February Through May."

Pre-publication review of *V. Publishers Weekly,* 28 January 1963, 189.

"Opportunities and Awards." *Cornell Daily Sun,* 28 May 1959, 7.

Ozier, Lance W. "Antipointsmen/Antimexico: Some Mathematical Imagery in *Gravity's Rainbow.*" *Critique* 16, no. 2 (1974): 73-90.

————. "The Calculus of Transformation: More Mathematical Imagery in *Gravity's Rainbow.*" *Twentieth Century Literature* 21 (May 1975): 193-210.

Page, Tim. " 'Genius Grant' for Pynchon." *Newsday,* 20 July 1988, sec. 2: 9, 14.

Palmeri, Frank. "Neither Literally nor as Metaphor: Pynchon's *The Crying of Lot 49* and the Structure of Scientific Revolutions." *ELH* 54 (1987): 979-99.

"Paperbacks of the Month." *New York Times Book Review,* 10 March 1974, 28, 30.

Parr, John. "Pynchon's First Flights." Review of *Slow Learner. Toronto Star,* 16 June 1984, M4.

Patteson, Richard. "What Stencil Knew: Structure and Certitude in Pynchon's *V.*" *Critique* 16, no. 2 (1974): 30-43.

————. "Architecture and Junk in Pynchon's Short Fiction." *Illinois Quarterly* 42, no. 2 (Winter 1979): 38-47.

————. "Horus, Harmakhis and Harpokrates in Chapter III of *V.* and 'Under the Rose.' " *Pynchon Notes* 6 (June 1981): 39-40.

————. "How True a Text? Chapter Three of *V.* and 'Under the Rose.' " *Southern Humanities Review* 18 (Fall 1984): 299-308.

Pearce, Richard. Review of *The Crying of Lot 49.* In *Survey of Contemporary Literature, Revised Edition,* edited by Frank N. Magill. Englewood Cliffs, New Jersey: Salem Press, 1977. 3:1662-65.

———. "The Sixties: Fiction in Fact." *Novel* 11 (Winter 1978): 163-72.

———. Review of Plater (1978). *Studies in American Fiction* 7 (1979): 110-12.

———. "Thomas Pynchon & the Novel of Motion: Where're They At, Where're They Going?" *Massachusetts Review* 21 (Spring 1980): 177-95. Reprinted as "Where're They At, Where're They Going? Thomas Pynchon and the American Novel in Motion" in Pearce (1981), 213-29. Reprinted under original title in his *The Novel in Motion: An Approach to Modern Fiction.* Columbus: Ohio State University Press, 1983. 83-107.

———. "Thomas Pynchon: 1937- ." In *American Writers: A Collection of Literary Biographies,* edited by A. Walton Litz. New York: Scribner's, 1982. Supplement II, part 2, 617-38.

———. "Richard Pearce Replies." *Pynchon Notes* 17 (Fall 1985): 51.

———. "Pynchon's Endings." *Novel* 18 (Winter 1985): 145-53.

———. "What Joyce after Pynchon?" In *Joyce: The Centennial Symposium,* edited by Morris Beja, et al. Urbana: University of Illinois Press, 1986. 43-46.

———, ed. *Critical Essays on Thomas Pynchon.* Boston: G.K. Hall, 1981.

Pearson, Carol S. "Puritans, Literary Critics, and Thomas Pynchon's *The Crying of Lot 49.*" *Notes on Contemporary Literature* 8, no. 2 (1978): 8-9.

———. "The Shadow Knows: Jung, Pynchon, and *The Crying of Lot 49.*" *Higginson Journal of Poetry* 20 (1978): 29-45.

———, and Katherine Pope. "The Emperor's New Clothes: The Fortunate Fall." Chap. 5 of *The Female Hero in American and British Literature.* New York: Bowker, 1981. 154-60.

Peirce, Carol Marshall. "Teaching Pynchon to Undergraduates." CEA Seminar, 3 April 1981. Published as "Pynchon's *V.* and Durrell's *Alexandria Quartet:* A Seminar in the Modern Tradition." *Pynchon Notes* 8 (February 1982): 23-27.

Peper, Jürgen. "Postmodernismus: 'Unitary Sensibility.'" *Amerikastudien* 22, no. 1 (1977): 65-89.

Peterson, Clarence. "Personal Choices for Personal Pleasure." Review of *V. Chicago Tribune Books Today,* 28 February 1965, 13.

—. "Some of the Best." Review of *The Crying of Lot 49. Chicago Tribune Books Today,* 7 May 1967, 9.

Petillon, Pierre-Yves. "Thomas Pynchon et l'espace aléatoire." *Critique* 34, no. 379 (1978): 1107-42. Reprinted in *La grand-route: Espace et écriture en Amérique.* Paris: Seuil, 1979. 179-229. Translated by Margaret S. Langford with Clifford Mead as "Thomas Pynchon and Aleatory Space." *Pynchon Notes* 15 (Fall 1984): 3-46.

—. "American Graffiti: S=k log W." Review of *L'Homme qui apprenait lentement* (D4a) and *Entropy/Entropie* (D11). *Critique* 41, no. 462 (November 1985): 1090-1105.

—. "Integrales de l'Arc-en-ciel." *Le Journal litteraire* (1988): 6-9.

Philip, Neil. Review of Tanner (1982). *British Book News,* October 1982, 639.

Phillips, William. "Notes on the New Style." *Nation,* 20 September 1965, 232-36. Reprinted in *The American Novel Since World War II,* edited by Marcus Klein. Greenwich, Connecticut: Fawcett, 1969. 252-61.

"Pieces of What?" Review of *V. Times Literary Supplement,* 11 October 1963, 813.

Plater, William M. *The Grim Phoenix: Reconstructing Thomas Pynchon.* Bloomington, Indiana: Indiana University Press, 1978.

—. Review of Cowart (1980). *South Atlantic Review* 46 (January 1981): 134-38.

Plimpton, George. "Mata Hari with a Clockwork Eye, Alligators in the Sewer." Review of *V. New York Times Book Review,* 21 April 1963, 5.

Plott, David A. "Eccentric Writers." *American Literary Almanac: From 1608 to the Present,* edited by Karen L. Rood. New York: Facts on File, 1988. 250.

Poenicke, Klaus. "Jenseits von Puer und Senex: der Pikaro und die Figurenphänomenologie der Postmoderne." *Amerikastudien* 24 (1979): 221-45. Reprinted as "Senex, Puer, Pikaro und Pynchons *Enden der Parabel*" in Ickstadt (1981), 228-54.

———. "Violence, Body, Text: The Hazards of an Ecological Hermeneutic." *Discourse* 9 (1987): 4-23 (16-17).

Poirier, Richard. "Introduction." In *Prize Stories 1962: The O. Henry Awards.* Garden City, New York: Doubleday, 1962. 7-15.

———. "Cook's Tour." Review of *V. New York Review of Books,* June 1963, 32.

———. "Embattled Underground." Review of *The Crying of Lot 49. New York Times Book Review,* 1 May 1966, 5, 42-43.

———. *A World Elsewhere: The Place of Style in American Literature.* New York: Oxford University Press, 1966. 250-52.

———. "The Politics of Self-Parody." *Partisan Review* 35 (Summer 1968): 339-53. Reprinted in *The Performing Self.* New York: Oxford University Press, 1971. 27-44.

———. "A Literature of Law and Order." *Partisan Review* 36 (1969): 189-204. Reprinted in *The Performing Self,* 3-26.

———. "Rocket Power." Review of *Gravity's Rainbow. Saturday Review of the Arts,* 1 March 1973, 59-64. Reprinted in Mendelson (1978), 167-78, and in Bloom (1986b), 11-20. Also reprinted as "Literary Rocketry of Thomas Pynchon." *Dialog* [Warsaw, Poland] 9, no. 1 (1976): 64-65.

———. "The Importance of Thomas Pynchon." *Twentieth Century Literature* 21, no. 2 (May 1975): 151-62. Reprinted in Levine and Leverenz (1976), 15-29, and in Bloom (1986a), 47-58.

———. "The Difficulties of Modernism and the Modernism of Difficulty." In *Images and Ideas in American Culture: The Functions of Criticism, Essays in Memory of Philip Rahv,* edited by Arthur Edelstein. Hanover, New Hampshire: Brandeis University Press, 1979. 124-40.

———. "Humans." Review of *Slow Learner. London Review of Books,* 24 January 1985, 18-20.

———. [See under Taylor, Benjamin.]

Polek, Fran. "Temporal Fragmentation and Identity in Some Post-Modern Novels." *Greyfriar* 20 (1980): 35-43.

Pollock, Venetia. Review of *V. Punch,* 13 November 1963, 722-23.

Pops, Martin Leonard. "Perpetual Motions." *Salmagundi* 38-39 (1977): 80-99.

Porush, David. Review of Plater (1978). *American Book Review* 2, no. 3 (1980): 16.

———. "Technology and Postmodernism: Cybernetic Fiction." *Sub-Stance* 27 (Fall 1980): 92-100. Reprinted in *The Soft Machine: Cybernetic Fiction.* New York: Methuen, 1984.

———. "Reading in the Servo-Mechanical Loop: The Machinery of Metaphor in Pynchon's Fictions." Chap. 6 of *The Soft Machine,* 112-35.

Powers, John. "Peeping at Tom: The Search for the Elusive Pynchon." *City Paper* [Baltimore, Maryland], 11 May 1984, 18-19.

Powers, Thomas. "Of Several Minds (Cont.)." *Commonweal,* 4 June 1982, 328-29.

Prescott, Peter S. "The Collegiate Pynchon." Review of *Slow Learner. Newsweek,* 9 April 1984, 100-101.

Price, Penelope. "Between the One and the Zero." Paper presented at the Rocky Mountain Modern Language Association's Pynchon seminar, October 1978.

———. "Pynchon's Wild West Projection." Paper presented at the Southwest Popular Culture Association, February 1980.

———. Review of Cowart (1980). *Rocky Mountain Review* 35, no. 1 (1981): 155-57.

———. " 'The Komical Kamikazes': Dying of Laughter in *Gravity's Rainbow.*" In *The Language of Humor/ The Humor of Language: Proceedings of the 1982 WHIM Conference,* edited by Don L. F. Nilsen. Tempe, Arizona: Western Humor and Irony Membership, 1983. 101-2.

Price, R. G. G. Review of *The Crying of Lot 49. Punch,* 26 April 1967, 618.

Pritchard, William. "Theatre of Operations." Review of *Gravity's Rainbow. New Statesman,* 16 November 1973, 734-35.

———. "Novels and Novelists in the 1960's." In *Modern Occasions 1: New Fiction, Criticism, Poetry,* edited by Philip Rahv. Port Washington, N.Y.: Kennikat, 1974. 188-209 (206-8).

Profit, Marie-Claude. "La Rhètorique de la mort dans *The Crying of Lot 49." Delta* 8 (1979): 155-74. Translated by Margaret S. Langford as "The Rhetoric of Death in *The Crying of Lot 49." Pynchon Notes* 10 (October 1982): 18-36.

Protebi, John. "Pynchon, Thomas." *World Authors: 1950-1970,* edited by John Wakeman. New York: Wilson, 1975: 1175-76.

———. "Pynchon, Thomas." *Current Biography Yearbook: 1987,* edited by Charles Moritz. New York: H.W. Wilson, 1988. 450-54. Reprinted from *Current Biography,* October 1987, 39-42.

"The Pulitzer Flap." *Time,* 20 May 1974, 61.

Punter, David. *The Literature of Terror: A History of Gothic Fictions from 1765 to the Present Day.* London: Longman, 1980. 373-74, 389-94, 400, 403-5, 407.

Purdy, S. B. "The Electronic Novel." *New Orleans Review* 9, no. 2 (Fall 1982): 26-33.

Pütz, Manfred. "Thomas Pynchon's *The Crying of Lot 49:* The World Is a Tristero System." *Mosaic* 7, no. 4 (Summer 1974): 125-37.

———. "Imagination and Self-Definition." *Partisan Review* 44 (1977): 235-44.

———. "Thomas Pynchon: History, Self, and the Narrative Discourse." In *The Story of Identity: American Fiction of the Sixties.* Stuttgart: Metzlersche Verlagsbuchhandlung, 1979. 130-57.

———. "Thomas Pynchon's *V.:* Geschichtserfahrung und narrativer Diskurs." In Ickstadt (1981), 75-103.

———, and Alan J. Friedman. "Science as Metaphor: Thomas Pynchon and *Gravity's Rainbow.*" *Contemporary Literature* 15 (Summer 1974): 345-59. Reprinted in Bloom (1986a), 23-35.

"Pynchon, Singer Share Fiction Prize." *New York Times,* 17 April 1974, 37.

Pyuen, Carolyn S. "The Transmarginal Leap: Meaning and Process in *Gravity's Rainbow.*" *Mosaic* 15, no. 2 (June 1982): 33-46.

Qazi, Javaid. "Source Material for Thomas Pynchon's Fiction: An Annotated Bibliography." *Pynchon Notes* 2 (February 1980): 7-19.

———. "Pynchon in Central Asia: The Use of Sources and Resources." *Rocky Mountain Review* 34, no. 4 (Fall 1980): 229-42.

Quilligan, Maureen. *The Language of Allegory: Defining the Genre.* Ithaca: Cornell University Press, 1979. 42-46, 204-23, 261-63, 265-78, 289-90. Reprinted, with slight adaptation, as "Thomas Pynchon and the Language of Allegory" in Pearce (1981), 187-212, and in Bloom (1986a), 111-37.

Raddatz, Fritz J. "Todes-Zeugung." Review of *Die Enden der Parabel* (D3d) and Ickstadt (1981). *Die Zeit,* 9 April 1982, 28.

Rankin, Ian J. "A Historicist Approach to Pynchon." Review of Nicholson and Stevenson (1984). *Pynchon Notes* 16 (1985): 110-11.

Rawson, Claude. "Ex post facto Fictions." Review of Tanner (1982). *Times Literary Supplement,* 3 September 1982, 941-42.

"Reading Blitz for Pynchon Work." *Boston Globe,* 17 February 1981, 21.

Redfield, Robert, and Peter L. Hays. "Fugue as a Structure in Pynchon's 'Entropy.' " *Pacific Coast Philology* 12 (1977): 50-55.

Reitz, Bernhard. " 'A Very German Question': Der Mitläufer als Voyeur und als Opfer in Pynchon's *V.* und *Gravity's Rainbow.*" *Anglistik & Englischunterricht 1986* 29-30 (1986): 173-98.

Review of Clerc (1983). *Antioch Review* 41 (Summer 1983): 371-72.

———. *Choice* 20 (June 1983): 1450-52.

Review of Cooper (1983). *Choice* 21 (October 1983): 272-74.

Review of Cowart (1980). *Choice* 18 (October 1980): 242.

Review of *The Crying of Lot 49. Choice* 3 (January 1967): 1017.

———. *Kirkus Reviews* 34 (January 1966): 28.

———. *Newsweek,* 2 May 1966, 104-5.

———. *Playboy,* April 1966, 25-26.

———. *Publishers Weekly,* 13 March 1967, 62.

———. *Virginia Quarterly Review* 42, no. 3 (Summer 1966): lxxxviii.

Review of Fowler (1981). *Choice* 18 (April 1981): 1097.

Review of *Gravity's Rainbow. Booklist* 69 (1 June 1973): 930.

———. *Choice* 10 (June 1973): 622-23.

———. *Kirkus Reviews* 40 (15 December 1972): 1443.

———. *Observer,* 3 November 1974, 29.

———. *Progressive,* February 1974, 66.

———. *Publishers Weekly,* 8 January 1973, 62.

———. *Virginia Quarterly Review* 49, no. 3 (Summer 1973): civ.

Review of Hite (1983). *Choice* 21 (February 1984): 822.

Review of Mendelson (1978). *Choice* 15 (September 1978): 872, 874.

Review of Pearce (1981). *Choice* 19 (February 1982): 763-64.

———. *Times Literary Supplement,* 20 November 1981, 1373.

Review of Plater (1978). *Choice* 15 (December 1978): 1372.

———. *Virginia Quarterly Review* 55, no. 2 (Spring 1979): 48.

Review of Schaub (1981). *Choice* 19 (September 1981): 82.

———. *Library Journal* 106 (15 April 1981): 884.

Review of Seigel (1978). *Choice* 15 (February 1979): 1668.

Review of *Slow Learner*. *Kirkus Reviews,* 1 February 1984, 106.

———. *Publishers Weekly,* 17 February 1984, 72.

———. *New Yorker,* 23 April 1984, 130.

Review of Stark (1980). *Antioch Review* 40 (Winter 1982): 120.

———. *Choice* 18 (December 1980): 533.

Review of Tanner (1982). *Choice* 20 (October 1982): 270.

Review of *V*. *Observer,* 5 June 1966, 22.

———. *Publishers Weekly,* 21 January 1963, 97.

———. *Virginia Quarterly Review* 39, no. 3 (Summer 1963): lxxxviii.

Richard, Claude. "Causality and Mimesis in Contemporary Fiction." *Sub-Stance* 40 (1983): 84-93.

———. "Le Graal du référent." *Fabula* 2 (1983): 9-27.

———. "Oedipa Regina." *Dires* [Montpellier, France] 2 (1984): 67-83.

Richardson, Robert O. "The Absurd Animate in Thomas Pynchon's *V.: A Novel.*" *Studies in the Twentieth Century* 9 (Spring 1972): 35-58.

Richer, Carol F. "The Prismatic Character of *Gravity's Rainbow.*" *Pynchon Notes* 12 (June 1983): 26-38.

Richter, David. "The Failure of Completeness: Pynchon's *V.*" In *Fable's End: Completeness and Closure in Rhetorical Fiction.* Chicago: University of Chicago Press, 1974. 101-35, 199-200.

Richwell, Adrian Emily. *"The Crying of Lot 49:* A Source Study." *Pynchon Notes* 17 (Fall 1985): 78-80.

———. "Pynchon's *The Crying of Lot 49." Explicator* 47, no. 1 (Fall 1988): 50-52.

Ricks, Christopher. "Voluminous." Review of *V. New Statesman,* 11 October 1963, 492.

Riese, Utz. "Thomas Pynchon: Antimonopolist Perspectives in Post-modernist Fiction." *Wissenschaftliche Zeitschrift der Humboldt-Universität zu Berlin* 33 (1984): 455-56.

Riley, Carolyn, and Thomas Harte, eds. *Contemporary Literary Criticism: Excerpts from Criticism of the Works of Today's Novelists, Poets, Playwrights, and Other Creative Writers.* Detroit: Gale Research, 1974. 2:253-58; 1976, 3:408-20.

Riley, Carolyn, and Phyllis Carmel Menderson, eds. *Contemporary Literary Criticism: Excerpts from Criticism of the Works of Today's Novelists, Poets, Playwrights, and Other Creative Writers.* Detroit: Gale Research, 1976. 6:430-39.

Roeder, Bill. "After the Rainbow." *Newsweek,* 7 August 1978, 17.

Rogers, W.G. Review of *Gravity's Rainbow. New York Post,* 27 February 1973.

Rose, Alan Henry. *Demonic Vision: Racial Fantasy and Southern Fiction.* Hamden, Conn.: Shoestring, 1976. 130, 132-34.

Rose, Remington. "At Home with Oedipa Maas." Review of *The Crying of Lot 49. New Republic,* 14 May 1966, 39-40.

Rosenbaum, Jonathan. "One Man's Meat is Another Man's Poisson." *Village Voice,* 29 March 1973, 24, 26.

———. "A Reply to F.S. Schwarzbach's 'Pynchon's Gravity' " *New Review,* July 1976, 64. Reprinted in Mendelson (1978), 67-68.

Rosenhein, Laurence. "Letter to Richard Pearce in Response to 'Pynchon's Endings.' " *Pynchon Notes* 17 (Fall 1985): 35-50.

Rosenthal, Raymond. "The Lost Treasure." Review of *The Crying of Lot 49. New Leader,* 23 May 1966, 21-22.

Ross, Alan. Review of *V. London Magazine* n.s. 3 (December 1963): 87.

Rother, James. "Parafiction: The Adjacent Universe of Barth, Barthelme, Pynchon, and Nabokov." *Boundary 2* 5 (Fall 1976): 21-43.

Rougé, Robert. "Histoire, psychanalyse et littérature chez trois romanciers américains contemporains: Warren, Styron, Pynchon." In *Exchanges: actes du congrès de Strasbourg.* Paris: Didier, 1982. 393-403.

Rovit, Earl. "Some Shapes in Recent American Fiction." *Contemporary Literature* 15 (Summer 1974): 539-61.

——. Review of Schaub (1981). *Library Journal* 106 (15 April 1981): 884-85.

Rubin, Louis D., Jr. "Two Lively Anthologies." *New York Times Book Review,* 18 March 1962, 31.

Russell, Charles. "The Vault of Language: Self-Reflective Artifice in Contemporary American Fiction." *Modern Fiction Studies* 20 (Autumn 1974): 349-59.

——. "Individual Voice in the Collective Discourse: Literary Innovation in Postmodern American Fiction." *Sub-Stance* 27 (1980): 29-39.

——. "Aporien der Postmoderne: Thomas Pynchon und die Schwerkraft der System." In Ickstadt (1981), 255-80; original English version "Pynchon's Language: Signs, Systems, and Subversion" in Clerc (1983), 251-72.

——. *Poets, Prophets, and Revolutionaries: The Literary Avant-Garde from Rimbaud through Postmodernism.* New York: Oxford University Press, 1985. 249, 253, 260-62, 264, 266-68.

Ryf, Robert S. "Character and Imagination in the Experimental Novel." *Modern Fiction Studies* 20 (Autumn 1974): 317-27.

Sabri, M. Arjamand. "Salute to Death." Review of *Gravity's Rainbow*. *Prairie Schooner* 47 (Fall 1973): 269-70.

Safer, Elaine B. "The Allusive Mode and Black Humor in Barth's *Giles Goat-Boy* and Pynchon's *Gravity's Rainbow*." *Renascence* 32, no. 2 (Winter 1980): 89-104. Revised and reprinted as "The Allusive Mode and Black Humor in Pynchon's *Gravity's Rainbow*" in Pearce (1981), 157-68.

———. "Teaching *Gravity's Rainbow* in 'The Contemporary American Epic Novel.'" CEA Seminar, 3 April 1981.

———. Review of Stark (1980). *Yearbook of English Studies* 13 (1983): 356-57.

———. *The Contemporary American Comic Epic: The Novels of Barth, Pynchon, Gaddis, and Kesey*. Detroit: Wayne State University Press, 1988. 79-110 and passim.

Salazar, Rothman. "Historicizing Phrenology: Wordsworth, Pynchon, and the Discursive Economy of the Cranial Text." *Raritan* 8, no. 1 (Summer 1988): 80-91.

Sale, Roger. "The Golden Age of the American Novel." *Ploughshares* 4, no. 3 (1978): 130-46.

———. "American Fiction in 1973." *Massachusetts Review* 14 (Autumn 1973): 834-46.

———. *On Not Being Good Enough: Writings of a Working Critic*. New York: Oxford University Press, 1979. 107-8, 133-36.

Sandbank, Shimon. "Parable and Theme: Kafka and American Fiction." *Comparative Literature* 37 (1985): 252-68.

Sanders, Scott. "Pynchon's Paranoid History." *Twentieth Century Literature* 21 (May 1975): 177-92. Reprinted in Levine and Leverenz (1976), 139-59. Translated by Piotr Kolyszko as "Pynchona historia paranoidalna" in *Literatura na Świecie*, 7/168 (1985): 246-69.

Sato, Yoshiaki. "Introduction to Thomas Pynchon." *Bokushin* 12 (1978): 112-17.

———. "Bunka o nugu koto, kigaeru koto: gendai amerika taiko-bunka bungaku ron" [On Undressing and Redressing Culture: An Essay on Contemporary American Countercultural Literature]. *Eigungak kenkyu* 55 (December 1978): 291-302.

———. "Thomas Pynchon o oritsumugu" [Embroidering Thomas Pynchon]. *Eureka* 11, no. 5 (December 1979): 195-205; 12, no. 2 (February 1980): 210-17; 12, no. 4 (April 1980): 170-79.

———. "Chitsujo to konton no arena de: Pynchon ni totte no katari" [The Arena Where Order Meets Chaos: On Pynchon's Narrative]. In *Bungaku to amerika: ohashi kenzaburo kyoju kanreki kinen robunshu.* Tokyo: Nan'un-do, 1980. 1:254-65.

———. "Pynchon in Japan: A Bibliography." *Pynchon Notes* 8 (February 1982): 61-62.

Saussy, George Stone, III. *The Oxter English Dictionary: Uncommon Words Used by Uncommonly Good Writers.* New York: Facts On File, 1984.

Schachterle, Lance. "Pynchon and Engineering Physics at Cornell." Paper presented at the 1988 Conference of the Society for Literature & Science. Albany, New York, 6-9 October 1988.

Schaub, Thomas Hill. "Open Letter in Response to Edward Mendleson's 'The Sacred, The Profane, and *The Crying of Lot 49.*'" *Boundary 2* 4 (Fall 1976): 93-101.

———. "Pynchon's Marvelous Style and the Finer Plot." American Literature Session 703, MLA Convention. Chicago, 30 December 1977.

———. *Pynchon: The Voice of Ambiguity.* Urbana: University of Illinois Press, 1981. Chap. 2 reprinted in Pearce (1981), 51-68.

———. "Where Have We Been, Where are We Headed?: A Retrospective Review of Pynchon Criticism." *Pynchon Notes* 7 (October 1981): 5-21.

———. "Thomas Pynchon." Review of Cooper (1983). *Contemporary Literature* 25 (1984): 260-62.

———. "*Slow Learner:* Good Writing Seems a Long Time Coming." *San Francisco Chronicle Review of Books,* 27 May 1984, 3, 9.

———. "Mythologies New and Old: Hume and Current Theory." Review

118

of Hume (1987). *Pynchon Notes* 18-19 (Spring-Fall 1986): 110-15.

Scheer-Schaezler, Brigitte. "Pynchon, Thomas." In *Encyclopedia of World Literature in the 20th Century,* edited by Wolfgang Bernard Fleischmann. New York: Frederick Ungar, 1971. 3:132-33.

———. "Language at the Vanishing Point: Some Notes on the Use of Language in Recent American Literature." *Revue des langues vivantes* 42 (1976): 497-508.

Schickel, Richard. "Paranoia at Full Cry." *World* 2, no. 8 (10 April 1973): 43-44.

Schmitz, Neil. "Describing the Demon: The Appeal of Thomas Pynchon." *Partisan Review* 42 (1975): 112-25.

Schoch, Mary Debra. "The Amazing Ithaca Literary Walking Tour." *Ithaca Journal,* 17 February 1984, 4-5.

Scholes, Robert. *Fabulation and Metafiction.* Urbana: University of Illinois Press, 1979. 4, 142, 206, 208-9.

Schuber, Stephen P. "Rereading Pynchon: Negative Entropy and 'Entropy.'" *Pynchon Notes* 13 (October 1983): 47-60.

———. "Textual Orbits/Orbiting Criticism: Deconstructing *Gravity's Rainbow.*" *Pynchon Notes* 14 (February 1984): 65-74.

Schulz, Max F. "Pop, Op, and Black Humor: The Aesthetics of Anxiety." *College English* 30 (December 1968): 230-41.

———. *Radical Sophistication: Studies in Contemporary Jewish-American Novelists.* Athens, Ohio: Ohio University Press, 1969. vii-viii.

———. "The Unconfirmed Thesis: Kurt Vonnegut, Black Humor, and Contemporary Art." *Critique* 12, no. 3 (1971): 5-28.

———. *Black Humor Fiction of the Sixties: A Pluralistic Definition of Man and His World.* Athens, Ohio: Ohio University Press, 1973. 61-64, 77-82, 143-45.

Schwab, Gabriele. "Creative Paranoia and Frost Patterns of White Words: Making Sense in and of Thomas Pynchon's *Gravity's Rainbow.*"

Center for Twentieth Century Studies: Working Paper No. 4 (Fall 1985): 1-19.

———. "Gravity's Rainbow oder die Lust an der Apokalyptischen Karvevalisierung des Heiligen Textes." Chap. 7 of Entgrenzungen und Entgrenzungsmythen: zur Subjektivitat im modernen Roman. Stuttgart: Franz Steiner Verlag Wiesbaden GmbH, 1987. 170-200.

Schwartz, Richard Alan. "Thomas Pynchon and the Evolution of Fiction." Science Fiction Studies 8, no. 2 (1981): 165-72.

———. "The Fantastic in Contemporary Fiction." In The Scope of the Fantastic: Theory, Technique, Major Authors, edited by Robert A. Collins and Howard D. Pearce. Westport, Connecticut: Greenwood, 1985. 27-32.

Schwartz, Tony. "Mixer of Elite and Pop." New York Times Book Review, 24 February 1980, 7.

Schwartzman, John. "Art, Science, and Change in Western Society." Ethos 5, no. 3 (1977): 239-62.

———. "Paradox, Play and Post-Modern Fiction." In Play and Culture, edited by Helen B. Schwartzman. West Point, New York: Leisure Press, 1980. 38-58.

Schwarzbach, F. S. "Pynchon's Gravity." New Review, June 1976, 39-42. Reprinted with revisions as "A Matter of Gravity" (editor's title) in Mendelson (1978), 56-78.

Scott, Nathan A., Jr. "The 'Conscience' of the New Literature." In The Shaken Realist: Essays in Modern Literature in Honor of Frederick J. Hoffman, edited by Melvin J. Friedman and John B. Vickery. Baton Rouge: Louisiana State University Press, 1970. 251-83.

Scotto, Robert M. Three Contemporary Novelists: An Annotated Bibliography of Works by and about John Hawkes, Joseph Heller, and Thomas Pynchon. New York: Garland, 1977. 93-132.

Seed, David. "The Fictional Labyrinths of Thomas Pynchon." Critical Quarterly 18, no. 4 (Winter 1976): 73-81.

———. Review of Plater (1978) and Siegel (1978). Journal of American Studies 14 (1980): 333-34.

———. "Pynchon's Two Tchitcherines." *Pynchon Notes* 5 (February 1981): 11-12.

———. "Order in Thomas Pynchon's 'Entropy.' " *Journal of Narrative Technique* 11, no. 2 (Spring 1981): 135-53. Reprinted in Bloom (1986a), 157-74.

———. "Pynchon's Names: Some Further Considerations." *Pynchon Notes* 6 (June 1981): 41-43.

———. Review of Stark (1980). *Journal of American Studies* 15 (August 1981): 296-97.

———. Review of Stark (1980). *Notes and Queries* 28 (1981): 468-69.

———. "Pynchon in Watts." *Pynchon Notes* 9 (June 1982): 54-60.

———. "Pynchon's Herero." *Pynchon Notes* 10 (October 1982): 37-44.

———. "Richard Fariña's Protest Novel." *Journal of American Culture* 5 (1982): 104-14.

———. "A Borrowing from Joyce in *The Crying of Lot 49.*" *Notes on Modern American Literature* 6, no. 3 (Winter 1982): item 17.

———. "The Central Asian Uprising of 1916." *Pynchon Notes* 11 (February 1983): 49-53.

———. Review of Tanner (1982). *Journal of American Studies* 17 (April 1983): 149-53.

———. "Pynchon's Textual Revisions of *The Crying of Lot 49.*" *Pynchon Notes* 12 (June 1983): 39-45.

———. "Fantasy and Dream in Thomas Pynchon's 'Low-lands.' " *Rocky Mountain Review of Language and Literature* 37, no. 1-2 (1983): 54-68.

———. "Understanding Pynchon." Review of Pearce (1981). *Essays in Criticism* 33 (1983): 75-78.

———. Review of Werner's *Paradoxical Resolutions: American Fiction Since James Joyce* and Clerc (1983). *Journal of American Studies* 17 (Winter 1983): 475-77.

———. Review of Cooper (1983) and Hite (1983). *Journal of American Studies* 18 (Summer 1984): 282-83.

———. "Thomas Hooker in Pynchon's *Gravity's Rainbow.*" *Notes on Modern American Literature* 8, no. 3 (1984): item 15.

———. "Further Notes and Sources for *Gravity's Rainbow.*" *Pynchon Notes* 16 (Spring 1985): 25-36.

———. "Naming in Pynchon and Joyce." In *James Joyce: The Centennial Symposium,* edited by Morris Beja, et al. Urbana: University of Illinois Press, 1986. 47-56.

———. *The Fictional Labyrinths of Thomas Pynchon.* London: Macmillan, 1988; Iowa City: University of Iowa Press, 1988.

Seidel, Michael. "The Satiric Plots of *Gravity's Rainbow.*" In Mendelson (1978), 193-212.

Seidenbaum, Art. "Endpapers." *Los Angeles Times Book Review,* 14 November 1982, 9.

"A Selected Vacation Reading List." *New York Times Book Review,* 10 June 1983, 39.

"A Selection of the Year's Best Books." *Time,* 31 December 1973, 56.

Serracino-Inglott, Peter. "The Faustus of Malta: An Interface of Fact and Fiction in Pynchon's *V.*" In *Individual and Community Commonwealth Literature,* edited by Daniel Massa. Msida: University of Malta Press, 1980. 224-37.

Seymour-Smith, Martin. *The New Guide to Modern World Literature.* New York: Macmillan, 1985. 146.

Shapiro, Stephen A. "The Ambivalent Animal: Man in the Contemporary British and American Novel." *Centennial Review* 12 (1968): 1-22.

Shattuck, Roger. "Fiction à la Mode." Review of *The Crying of Lot 49. New York Review of Books,* 23 June 1966, 22-24.

Sheppard, R. Z. "*V.* Squared." *Time,* 5 March 1973, 74-75.

———. "Business as Usual." Review of William Gaddis' *J R. Time,* 13

October 1975, 98.

Sherrill, Rowland A. "The Bible and Twentieth Century American Fiction." In *The Bible and American Arts and Letters,* edited by Giles Gunn. Philadelphia: Fortress, 1983. 57-82.

Shimura, Masao. "Thomas Pynchon Note." *Eigo Seinen* 120 (1975): 458-59.

————. "Gendai amerika no gothic shosetsu: Thomas Pynchon no baai" [Thomas Pynchon: A Contemporary American Gothicist]. *Bokushin* 1 (1975): 166-70.

————. "Kataui, plot, Pynchon" [Deception, Plot, Pynchon]. *Gendaishi techo* 21, no. 5 (May 1978): 50-56.

————. "Pynchon: hito to sakuhin—story to plot" [Pynchon and His Works: Story-Telling and Plot-Making]. *Umi* 10, no. 6 (June 1978): 314-28.

Shorris, Earl. "The Worldly Palimpsest of Thomas Pynchon." *Harper's,* June 1973, 78-80, 82.

Shrapnel, Norman. "Excursions into Strange Worlds." Review of *The Crying of Lot 49. Manchester Guardian Weekly,* 20 April 1967, 11.

Siegel, Jules. "The Dark Triumvirate." *Cavalier,* August 1965, 14-16, 90-91.

————. "Who Is Thomas Pynchon . . . And Why Did He Take Off with My Wife?" *Playboy,* March 1977, 97, 122, 168-70, 172, 174.

Siegel, Mark R. "Creative Paranoia: Understanding the System of *Gravity's Rainbow." Critique* 18, no. 3 (1977): 39-54.

————. "The Importance of Film in *Gravity's Rainbow.*" American Literature Session 703, MLA Convention. Chicago, 30 December 1977.

————. *Pynchon: Creative Paranoia in "Gravity's Rainbow."* Port Washington, New York: Kennikat Press, 1978.

————. "Pynchon's Anti-Quests." *Pynchon Notes* 3 (June 1980): 5-9.

————. "A Point Beyond Degree Zero: A Rebuttal to Khachig Tölölyan's

'Remarks' in *Pynchon Notes* 3." *Pynchon Notes* 4 (October 1980): 26-28.

―――. "Thomas Pynchon and the Science Fiction Controversy." *Pynchon Notes* 7 (October 1981): 38-42.

―――. "Contemporary Trends in Western American Fiction." In *A Literary History of the American West*, edited by Thomas J. Lyon, et al. Fort Worth: Texas Christian University Press, 1987. 1182-1201.

Siemens, William L. "Levity and Gravity in Pynchon's Rainbow." Paper presented at West Virginia University's Philological Society meeting, 12 March 1975.

Simberloff, Daniel. "Entropy, Information, and Life: Biophysics in the Novels of Thomas Pynchon." *Perspectives in Biology and Medicine* 21 (Summer 1978): 617-25.

Simmon, Scott. "*Gravity's Rainbow* Described." *Critique* 16, no. 2 (1974): 54-67; "A Character Index: *Gravity's Rainbow*," 68-72.

―――. "Beyond the Theatre of War: *Gravity's Rainbow* as Film." *Literature/Film Quarterly* 6 (1977): 347-63. Reprinted in Pearce (1981), 124-39.

Simons, John L. "Third Story Man: Biblical Irony in Thomas Pynchon's 'Entropy.'" *Studies in Short Fiction* 14 (Winter 1977): 88-93.

―――. "Pynchon on Household: Reworking the Traditional Spy Novel." *Pynchon Notes* 16 (Spring 1985): 83-88.

Sissman, L. E. "Hieronymus and Robert Bosch: The Art of Thomas Pynchon." Review of *Gravity's Rainbow*. *New Yorker,* 19 May 1973, 138-40.

Skarzenski, Donald. "Enzian and the Octopus: Fact in Pynchon's Fiction." *Notes on Modern American Literature* 1, no. 4 (Fall 1977): item 35.

Skerrett, Joseph Taylor, Jr. "Dostoievsky, Nathaneal [*sic*] West, and Some Contemporary American Fiction." *University of Dayton Review* 4, no. 1 (1967): 23-35.

Sklar, Robert. "The New Novel, USA: Thomas Pynchon." *Nation,* 25 September 1967, 277-80. Reprinted as "The Anarchist Miracle: The

Novels of Thomas Pynchon" (editor's title) in Mendelson (1978), 87-96.

Slade, Joseph W. *Thomas Pynchon.* New York: Warner Paperback Library, 1974. Revised version of Chap. 1 reprinted as " 'Entropy' and Other Calamities" in Mendelson (1978), 69-86.

————. "Pynchon as a Technological Humanist." American Literature Special Session 388, MLA Convention. New York, 28 December 1976.

————. "Escaping Rationalization: Options for the Self in *Gravity's Rainbow.*" *Critique* 18, no. 3 (1977): 27-38.

————. "Thomas Pynchon: Postindustrial Humanist." *Technology and Culture* 23, no. 1 (January 1982): 53-72.

————. "From Cabals to Post-Structural Kabbalah." Review of Tanner (1982). *Pynchon Notes* 10 (October 1982): 58-62.

————. "Thomas Pynchon." In *American Writing Today,* edited by Richard Kostelanetz. Washington, D.C.: International Communication Agency Forum Series, 2, 1982. 211-22.

————. "Religion, Psychology, Sex, and Love in *Gravity's Rainbow.*" In Clerc (1983), 153-98.

————. "Pynchon Studies Fifteen Years after *Gravity's Rainbow.*" Paper presented at the 1988 Conference of the Society for Literature & Science. Albany, New York, 6-9 October 1988.

Slatoff, Walter. Review of *V. Epoch* 12, no. 4 (Spring 1963): 255-57.

Sloan, James Park. "Pynchon's Evasive New Novel." Review of *Gravity's Rainbow. Chicago Sun-Times Book Week,* 18 March 1973, 19.

Slung, Michele. "Book Report: Early Pynchon." Review of *Slow Learner. Book World,* 11 March 1984, 15.

Smetak, Jacqueline. "Thomas Pynchon's 'Mortality and Mercy in Vienna': Major Themes in an Early Work." *Iowa Journal of Literary Studies* 4, no. 1 (1983): 65-76.

Smith, H. Allen. "Just Who Is J. D. Salinger?" *Playboy,* January 1966, 165, 248.

Smith, Mack. "The Paracinematic Reality of *Gravity's Rainbow.*" *Pynchon Notes* 9 (June 1982): 17-37.

Smith, Marcus. "*Gravity's Rainbow:* A Jeremiad for Now." American Literature Session 703, MLA Convention. Chicago, 30 December 1977.

————. "*V.* and *The Maltese Falcon:* A Connection?" *Pynchon Notes* 2 (February 1980): 6.

————, and Khachig Tölölyan. "The New Jeremiad: *Gravity's Rainbow.*" In Pearce (1981), 169-86. Reprinted in Bloom (1986a), 139-55.

Smith, Thomas S. "Performing in the Zone: The Presentation of Historical Crisis in *Gravity's Rainbow.*" *CLIO* 12 (Spring 1983): 245-60.

Solberg, Sara M. "On Comparing Apples and Oranges: James Joyce and Thomas Pynchon." *Comparative Literature Studies* 16, no. 1 (March 1979): 33-40.

Solomon, Charlotte D. "Recovering World War II: Film and *Gravity's Rainbow.*" Paper presented at the Florida State University Comparative Literature Circle Conference on Literature and Film, January 1981.

Soonckindt, Louis. "Postface." In *Entropy/Entropie* (D11), 41-69.

Soules, Terrill Shepard. "What to Think about *Gravity's Rainbow.*" *Esquire,* October 1980, 104-7.

Spanos, William V. *Repetitions: The Postmodern Occasion in Literature and Culture.* Baton Rouge: Louisiana State University Press, 1987. 170, 182, 261, 275.

Spilka, Mark. "Character as a Lost Cause," *Novel* 11 (Spring 1978): 197-217.

Spirer, Ellen. " 'Candidates for Survival': A Talk with Harold Bloom." *Boston Review,* February 1986, 12-13.

Sprinker, Michael. "Entropy." In *Masterplots II: Short Story Series,* edited by Frank N. Magill. Englewood Cliffs, N.J.: Salem Press, 1986. 2:709-11.

Staley, Robert. "The New Science in the New Classics: Pynchon, Barth and Coover." Paper presented at the Colorado Seminars in Literature, April 1981.

Stark, John. "The Arts and Sciences of Thomas Pynchon." *Hollins Critic* 12, no. 4 (October 1975): 1-13.

———. "Thomas Pynchon." In *Dictionary of Literary Biography; Volume Two: American Novelists Since World War II*, edited by Jeffrey Helterman and Richard Layman. Detroit: Gale Research, 1978. 411-17.

———. *Pynchon's Fictions: Thomas Pynchon and the Literature of Information.* Athens, Ohio: Ohio University Press, 1980.

Steiner, Wendy. "Collage or Miracle: Historicism in a Deconstructed World." In *Reconstructing American Literary History*, edited by Sacvan Bercovitch. Cambridge: Harvard University Press, 1986, 323-51.

Stern, Jerome H. "The Interfaces of *Gravity's Rainbow.*" *Dismisura* 39-50 (1980): 51-57.

Stevick, Philip. "Lies, Fiction, and Mock Facts." *Western Humanities Review* 30 (Winter 1976): 1-12.

Stickney, John. "A Reader's Guide to Thomas Pynchon." *Mademoiselle,* December 1974, 27, 38.

Stimpson, Catherine R. "Pre-Apocalyptic Atavism: Thomas Pynchon's Early Fiction." In Levine and Leverenz (1976), 31-47. Reprinted in Bloom (1986a), 79-81.

Stoltzfus, Ben. "The Aesthetics of *Nouveau Roman* and Innovative Fiction." *International Fiction Review* 10, no. 2 (1983): 108-16.

Stonehill, Brian. "A Trestle of Letters." *Fiction International* 12 (1980): 259-68.

———. *The Self-Conscious Novel: Artifice in Fiction from Joyce to Pynchon.* Philadelphia: University of Pennsylvania Press, 1988. 141-56, 184, 188-90 and passim.

Storey, Philip. "William Slothrop: Gentleman." *Pynchon Notes* 13

(October 1983): 61-70.

Stovkis, Irene. "Books to Come." Prepublication notice of *V.* announcing 20 March 1963 as publication date. *Library Journal* 88 (1 February 1963): 629.

Stowe, William W. "Confronting Mystery with Method." Review of Tani's *The Doomed Detective. Pynchon Notes* 15 (Fall 1984): 86-90.

Strawson, Galen. "Study-aids from Another Planet." Review of *Slow Learner. Times Literary Supplement,* 11 January 1985, 41.

Strehle, Susan. "Actualism: Pynchon's Debt to Nabokov." *Contemporary Literature* 24 (Spring 1983): 30-50.

———. Review of Cowart (1980) and Stark (1980). *Style* 17, no. 1 (Winter 1983): 84-86.

Styron, William. "Presentation to Thomas Pynchon of the Howells Medal for Fiction of the Academy." *Proceedings of the American Academy of Arts and Letters and the National Institute of Arts and Letters,* second series, no. 26 (1976): 43-46.

Suguira, Ginsaku. "Nature, History, and Entropy: A Reading of Faulkner's *Absalom, Absalom!* in comparison with *Moby-Dick* and *V." William Faulkner: Materials, Studies and Criticism* 2, no. 2 (1979): 21-33.

Sullivan, Phil. *"Gravity's Rainbow."* In *Survey of Contemporary Literature: Revised Edition,* edited by Frank N. Magill. Englewood Cliffs, New Jersey: Salem Press, 1977. 5:3087-91.

Swanson, Roy Arthur. "Versions of Doublethink in *Gravity's Rainbow, Darkness Visible, Riddley Walker* and *Travels to the Enu." World Literature Today* 58, no. 2 (Spring 1984): 203-8.

Swartzlander, Susan. "The Tests of Reality: The Use of History in *Ulysses* and *Gravity's Rainbow." Critique* 29, no. 2 (Winter 1988): 133-43.

Swigger, Ronald T. "Fictional Encyclopedism and the Cognitive Value of Literature." *Comparative Literature Studies* 12 (December 1975): 351-66.

Tabbi, Joseph. "Pynchon's 'Entropy.' " *Explicator* 43 (Fall 1984): 61-63.

——. "Merging Orders: The Shaping Influence of Science on 'Entropy.' " *Pynchon Notes* 15 (Fall 1984): 58-68.

——. "Science and Engineering in Recent Pynchon Criticism." Paper presented at the 1988 Conference of the Society for Literature & Science. Albany, New York, 6-9 October 1988.

Takács, Ferenc. "Models or Metaphors: Pattern and Paranoia in Pynchon's *The Crying of Lot 49.*" *Acta Litteraria Academiae Scientiarum Hungaricae* 23 (1981): 297-306.

Tani, Stefano. "The Dismemberment of the Detective." *Diogenes* 120 (Winter 1982): 22-41. Republished in slightly different format as part of chap. 4 in *The Doomed Detective: The Contribution of the Detective Novel to Postmodern American and Italian Fiction.* Carbondale: Southern Illinois University Press, 1984. 91-99.

Tanner, Tony. "The American Novelist as Entropologist." *London Magazine* n.s. 10, no. 7 (October 1970): 5-18. Reprinted as "Everything Running Down" in *City of Words: American Fiction 1950-1970.* New York: Harper and Row, 1971. 141-52.

——. "Patterns and Paranoia, or Caries and Cabals." *Salmagundi* 15 (1971): 78-99. Reprinted as "Caries and Cabals" in *City of Words,* 153-73, and reprinted in Levine and Leverenz (1976), 49-67.

——. "*V.* and V-2." *London Magazine* n.s. 13, no. 6 (February/March 1974): 80-88. Reprinted in Mendelson (1978), 47-55.

——. Review of Gaddis's *The Recognitions. New York Times Book Review,* 14 July 1974, 27-28.

——. "Games American Writers Play: Ceremony, Complicity, Contestation, and Carnival." *Salmagundi* 35 (Fall 1976): 110-40. Reprinted in *Scenes of Nature, Signs of Men.* Cambridge: Cambridge University Press, 1987. 176-205.

——. "Paranoia, Energy, and Displacement." *Wilson Quarterly* 2, no. 1 (Winter 1978): 143-50.

——. *Thomas Pynchon.* London: Methuen, 1982. Chap. 4 reprinted as ' *The Crying of Lot 49*" in Bloom (1986a), 175-89. Chap. 5 reprinted as "*Gravity's Rainbow:* An Experience in Modern Reading" in Bloom (1986b), 69-83.

Tate, J. O. "*Gravity's Rainbow:* The Original Soundtrack." *Pynchon Notes* 13 (October 1983): 3-24.

———. "Slow Burner." Review of *Slow Learner. National Review,* 16 November 1984, 53-55.

———. "A Note on Convergence." *Pynchon Notes* 15 (Fall 1984): 80-83.

Tatham, Campbell. "John Barth and the Aesthetics of Artifice." *Contemporary Literature* 12 (Winter 1971): 60-73.

———. "Tarot and *Gravity's Rainbow.*" *Modern Fiction Studies* 32 (1986): 581-90.

Taylor, Benjamin. "Negotiations: A Conversation with Richard Poirier." *Salmagundi* 52-53 (1981): 107-18.

Taylor, Gordon. Review of Schaub (1981). *American Literature* 54 (March 1982): 148-49.

Teitelbaum, Sheldon. "Cyberpunk: Out of Science Fiction, A New View of Contemporary Reality?" *Los Angeles Times,* 17 January 1985, 34.

Teltsch, Kathleen. "MacArthur Foundation Names 31 Recipients of 1988 Awards." *New York Times,* 19 July 1988, A23.

Thielemans, Johan. "Mba-Kayere and the Routes of Power: Pynchon's *Gravity's Rainbow* Read from Enzian's Point of View." In *American Literature in Belgium,* edited by Gilbert Debusscher. Amsterdam: Rodopi, 1987. 213-25.

Thigpen, Kenneth A. "Folklore in Contemporary American Literature: Thomas Pynchon's *V.* and the Alligators-in-the-Sewers Legend." *Southern Folklore Quarterly* 43, no. 1-2 (1979): 93-105.

Thiher, Allen. "Kafka's Legacy." *Modern Fiction Studies* 26 (Winter 1980-81): 543-62.

———. *Words in Reflection: Modern Language Theory and Postmodern Fiction.* Chicago: University of Chicago Press, 1984. 152-53.

"36 Prizes Awarded in Arts and Letters; Pynchon Rejects His." *New York Times,* 22 May 1975, 35.

Thomas, Brook. "What's the Point? On Comparing Joyce and Pynchon." *Pynchon Notes* 11 (February 1983): 44-48.

———. "Making Sense of One Brand of Modern Fiction." Review of Pearce's *The Novel in Motion. Boston Sunday Globe,* 23 October 1983, A-11.

Thomas, Claudine. "Une Parabole du pouvoir: Lecture de *The Crying of Lot 49,* de Thomas Pynchon." In *Le Discours de la violence dans la culture américaine,* edited by Régis Durand. Lille: Pubs. de l'Universite de Lille III, 1979. 119-38.

Thorburn, David. "A Dissent on Pynchon." *Commentary,* September 1973, 68-70.

Tillotson, T. S. "Gravitational Entropy in *Gravity's Rainbow." Pynchon Notes* 4 (October 1980): 23-24.

Tölölyan, Khachig. "Cold War and Hot Peace in *Gravity's Rainbow."* American Literature Special Session 388, MLA Convention. New York, 28 December 1976.

———. "Criticism as Symptom: Thomas Pynchon and the Crisis of the Humanities." *New Orleans Review* 5 (1977-78): 314-18.

———. "The Fishy Poisson: Allusions to Statistics in *Gravity's Rainbow." Notes on Modern American Literature* 4, no. 1 (1979): item 5.

———. "Prodigious Pynchon and His Progeny." Review essay of Siegel (1978) and Plater (1978). *Studies in the Novel* 11 (Summer 1979): 224-34.

———. "Some Remarks on Professor Mark Siegel's 'Pynchon's Anti-Quests.'" *Pynchon Notes* 3 (June 1980): 10-14.

———. Review of Schaub (1981). *Village Voice,* "Voice Literary Supplement," December 1981, 5.

———. "War as Background in *Gravity's Rainbow."* In Clerc (1983), 31-67.

———. "Seven on Pynchon: The Novelist as Deconstructionist." *Novel* 16 (Winter 1983): 165-72.

———. Review of *Slow Learner. Choice* 22 (September 1984): 100.

———. Review of Hayles's *The Cosmic Web. Modern Language Notes* 100 (1985): 1174-76.

———. "Pynchon, Thomas (1937-)." In *Postmodern Fiction: A Bio-Bibliographical Guide,* edited by Larry McCafferey. New York: Greenwood Press, 1986. 488-91.

———. Review of Hohmann (1986). *Choice* 25 (October 1987): 310.

———. Review of Moore (1987). *Choice* 25 (December 1987): 623.

———. "Discoursing with Culture: The Novel as Interlocutor." *Novel* 21 (Winter/Spring 1988): 228-38.

———, and Clay Leighton. *An Index to "Gravity's Rainbow."* Privately printed, Wesleyan University, 1980.

Trachtenberg, Stanley. "Beyond Initiation: Some Recent Novels." Review of *The Crying of Lot 49. Yale Review* 56 (Autumn 1966): 131-38.

———. "Counterhumor: Comedy in Contemporary American Fiction." *Georgia Review* 27 (Spring 1973): 33-48.

Tsurumi, Seiji. "Gendai shosetsu no ending: Pynchon, Barth, Brautigan." *Oberon* 45 (1982): 80-93.

Turpin, Michel. "Thomas Pynchon: *The Crying of Lot 49,* ou comment l'esprit vient au lecteur." *GRAAT* 2 (1985): 117-37.

Tylee, Claire M. "Thomas Pynchon: The Loss of Tragedy with the Spirit of Music." In *Los Ultimos veinte años en los estudios anglo-norte-americanos.* Actas del VIII congreso de AEDEAN. Málaga: University of Málaga, 1984. 145-50.

———. " 'Spot This Mumbo Jumbo': Thomas Pynchon's Emblems for American Culture in 'Mortality and Mercy in Vienna.' " *Revista canaria de estudios ingleses* 10 (April 1985): 141-56.

———. "Metaphor in the Early Fiction of Thomas Pynchon: A Study of

'Entropy.' " Actas del VII congreso de la AEDEAN. Madrid: Universidad Nacional de Educacion a Distancia, 1986. 219-25.

Ulm, Melvin, and David Holt. "The Zone and the Real: Philosophical Themes in *Gravity's Rainbow.*" *Pynchon Notes* 11 (February 1983): 27-43.

"*V* for Victory." Review of *V. Newsweek,* 1 April 1963, 82, 84.

"*V* Signs." *Times Literary Supplement,* 27 April 1967, 364.

Vauthier, Simone. "*Gravity's Rainbow* à la carte: Notes de lécture." *Fabula* 3 (March 1984): 97-118.

Vella, Michael W. "Pynchon, *V.,* and the French Surrealists." *Pynchon Notes* 18-19 (Spring-Fall 1986): 29-38.

Ventura, Michael. "Letters at 3 A.M.: Shop Talk." *LA Weekly,* 5-11 September 1986, 14.

Vester, Heinz-Günter. "Konjunktur der Konjekturen." *Demokratie und Sozialismus* 34 (1985): 11-28.

Vesterman, William. "Pynchon's Poetry." *Twentieth Century Literature* 21 (May 1975): 211-20. Reprinted in Levine and Leverenz (1976), 101-12.

Vidal, Gore. "American Plastic: The Matter of Fiction." *New York Review of Books,* 15 July 1976, 31-39. Reprinted in *Matters of Fact and of Fiction: Essays 1973-1976.* New York: Random House, 1977. 136-48.

———. "The Thinking Man's Novel." *New York Review of Books,* 4 December 1980, 10, 12, 14, 16, 19.

Wagner, Linda W. "A Note on Oedipa the Roadrunner." *Journal of Narrative Technique* 4, no. 2 (May 1974): 155-61.

"Waiting for the Bang." Review of *Gravity's Rainbow*. *Times Literary Supplement*, 16 November 1973, 1389.

Waldmeir, Joseph J. Review of Cowart (1980). *Modern Fiction Studies* 26 (Winter 1980-81): 675-81.

Walker, Robert H. "Patterns in Recent American Literature." In *American Character and Culture in a Changing World*, edited by John A. Hague. Westport, Connecticut: Greenwood, 1979. 65-80.

Wallace, Ronald. *The Last Laugh: Form and Affirmation in the Contemporary American Comic Novel*. Columbia, Missouri: University of Missouri Press, 1979. 11, 12, 15, 20, 24, 141.

Walsh, Thomas P., and Cameron Northouse. *John Barth, Jerzy Kosinski, and Thomas Pynchon: A Reference Guide*. Boston: G.K. Hall, 1977. 93-132, 143-45.

Walters, Ray. "Paperback Talk." *New York Times Book Review*, 15 February 1981, 35-36.

Warren, James Perrin. "Ritual Reluctance: The Poetics of Discontinuity in *Gravity's Rainbow*." *Pynchon Notes* 18-19 (Spring-Fall 1986): 55-65.

Wasson, Richard. "Notes on a New Sensibility." *Partisan Review* 36 (1969): 460-77. Reprinted in Pearce (1981), 113-19.

Watson, Robert N. "Who Bids for Tristero? The Conversion of Pynchon's Oedipa Maas." *Southern Humanities Review* 17 (Winter 1983): 59-75.

Watts, Harold H. "Pynchon, Thomas." *Great Writers of the English Language: Novelists and Prose Writers*, edited by James Vinson. New York: St. Martin's Press, 1979. 996-98. Reprinted with revisions in *Reference Guide to American Literature*, 2nd ed., edited by K. L. Kirkpatrick. Chicago and London: St. James Press, 1987. 450-51.

Waxler, Robert. "Two With Caution." Review of McConnell's *Four Postwar American Novelists* and Hendin's *Vulnerable People*. *Novel* 14 (Winter 1981): 179-83.

134

"We See You, Tom." 1955 photo of Pynchon. *New York,* 13 May 1974, 89.

Weber, Brom. "The Mode of 'Black Humor.' " *The Comic Imagination in American Literature,* edited by Louis D. Rubin, Jr. New Brunswick: Rutgers University Press, 1973. 361-71.

Weber, Donald. "West, Pynchon, Mailer, and the Jeremiad Tradition." *South Atlantic Quarterly* 83 (1984): 259-68.

Weinstein, Mark A. "The Creative Imagination in Fiction and History." *Genre* 9 (1976): 263-77.

Weisenburger, Steven. "Thomas Pynchon, Gödel's Theorem, the Rhetoric of Mathematics." Paper presented at the Modern Language Association convention, December 1977.

———. Review of Plater (1978). *Modern Language Quarterly* 40 (1979): 88-91.

———. "The End of History?: Thomas Pynchon and the Uses of the Past." *Twentieth Century Literature* 25 (Spring 1979): 54-72. Reprinted in Pearce (1981), 140-56.

———. "Contra Naturam?: Usury in William Gaddis' *J R.*" *Genre* 13 (1980): 93-109.

———. "The Origin of Pynchon's Tchitcherine." *Pynchon Notes* 8 (February 1982): 39-42.

———. "Paper Currencies: Reading William Gaddis." *Review of Contemporary Fiction* 2, no. 2 (1982): 12-22.

———. "Notes for *Gravity's Rainbow.*" *Pynchon Notes* 12 (June 1983): 3-15.

———. "The Chronology of Episodes in *Gravity's Rainbow.*" *Pynchon Notes* 14 (February 1984): 50-64.

———. Review of Hite (1983) and Cooper (1983). *Modern Fiction Studies* 30 (Summer 1984): 331-33.

———. "Pynchon's Hereros: A Textual and Bibliographical Note." *Pynchon Notes* 16 (Spring 1985): 37-45.

————. "Further Further Notes and Sources . . ." *Pynchon Notes* 17 (Fall 1985): 81-83.

————. *A "Gravity's Rainbow" Companion: Sources and Contexts for Pynchon's Novel.* Athens: University of Georgia Press, 1988.

Weisman, Steven R. "World of Books Presents Its Oscars." *New York Times,* 19 April 1974, 24.

Weixlmann, Joseph. "Thomas Pynchon: A Bibliography." *Critique* 14, no. 2 (1972): 34-43.

Wensberg, Erik. Review of *The Crying of Lot 49. Commonweal,* 8 July 1966, 446-48.

Werner, Craig. Review of Plater (1978), Siegel (1978), and Cowart (1980). *University of Mississippi Studies in English* n.s. 1 (1980): 155-59.

————. "Recognizing Reality, Realizing Responsibility: Joyce, Gaddis, and Pynchon." Chap. 5 of *Paradoxical Resolutions: American Fiction Since James Joyce.* Urbana: University of Illinois Press, 1982. 165-69, 181-94. Abridged version reprinted as "Recognizing Reality, Realizing Responsibility" in Bloom (1986a), 191-202, and in Bloom (1986b), 85-96.

Westervelt, Linda A. " 'A Place Dependent on Ourselves': The Reader as System-Builder in *Gravity's Rainbow." Texas Studies in Literature and Language* 22 (Spring 1980): 69-90.

"What Did You Think of NBA? An Informal Sampling of Opinion." *Publishers Weekly,* 13 May 1974, 40-41.

White, Allon. "Ironic Equivalence: A Reading of Thomas Pynchon's 'Mortality and Mercy in Vienna.' " *Critical Quarterly* 23 (Autumn 1981): 55-62.

————. "Pigs and Pierrots: The Politics of Transgression in Modern Fiction." *Raritan* 2, no. 2 (1982): 51-70.

————. "Bakhtin, Sociolinguistics and Deconstruction." In *The Theory of Reading,* edited by Frank Gloversmith. New York: Barnes & Noble, 1984. 123-46.

Wilde, Alan. "Irony in the Postmodern Age: Toward a Map of Suspensive-ness." *Boundary 2* 9 (Fall 1980): 5-46.

———. *Horizons of Assent: Modernism, Postmodernism, and the Ironic Imagination.* Baltimore: Johns Hopkins University Press, 1981. 47, 146-47, 165.

———. *Middle Grounds: Studies in Contemporary American Fiction.* Philadelphia: University of Pennsylvania Press, 1987. 75-103 and passim.

Willis, Ronald. "On Oddities." Review of *V. Books and Bookmen,* September 1966, 44-45.

Willis, Susan. "A Literary Lesson in Historical Thinking." *Social Text* 3 (1980): 136-43.

Wills, David, and Alec McHoul. " 'Die Welt ist alles was der Fall ist' (Wittgenstein, Weissman, Pynchon) / 'Le Signe est toujours le signe de la chute' (Derrida)." *Southern Review: Literary and Interdisciplinary Essays* 16 (July 1983): 274-91.

———. *"Gravity's Rainbow* and the Post-Rhetorical." *Southern Review* 19 (1986): 194-227.

Wilson, Raymond J., III. "Cozzens's *Guard of Honor* and Pynchon's *Gravity's Rainbow." Notes on Contemporary Literature* 9, no. 5 (1979): 6-8.

Wilson, Robert. "Fill Your Spring Book Bag with Top-Selling Authors." Review of *Slow Learner. USA Today,* 10 February 1984, D1.

Wilson, Robert Rawdon. "Spooking Oedipa: On Godgames." *Canadian Review of Comparative Literature* 4 (Spring 1977): 186-204.

———. "Godgames and Labyrinths: The Logic of Entrapment." *Mosaic* 15, no. 4 (December 1982): 1-22. Revised version of lecture entitled "In the Shadow of God's Prick: The Game of Labyrinths," presented at the annual Edmund Kemper Broadus Lectures at the University of Alberta, 1980.

Winkler, Willi. "Programm: Weltuntergang: Die frühen Erzählungen von Thomas Pynchon." *Merkur* 40 (April 1986): 337-39.

Winship, Kihm. *"Gravity's Rainbow:* An Index and Guide to Creative Works in Thomas Pynchon's Novel." Unpublished manuscript, Syracuse, New York, 1977.

Winston, Mathew. "The Quest for Pynchon." *Twentieth Century Literature* 21 (October 1975): 278-87. Reprinted in Levine and Leverenz (1976), 251-63. Translated by Jaroslaw Anders as "W poszukiwaniu Pynchona." *Literatura na Świecie* 6/62 (1976): 94-105.

———. "Critical Cornucopia." Review of Pearce (1981). *Pynchon Notes* 8 (February 1982): 47-53.

———. "A Comic Source of *Gravity's Rainbow.*" *Pynchon Notes* 15 (Fall 1984): 73-76.

Wolfe, Peter. *"Gravity's Rainbow."* *Studies in the Twentieth Century* 13 (Spring 1974): 125-28.

Wolff, Geoffrey. Review of *Gravity's Rainbow. Washington Post Bookworld,* 11 March 1973, 1-2.

Wolfley, Lawrence C. "Repression's Rainbow: The Presence of Norman O. Brown in Pynchon's Big Novel." *PMLA* 92 (October 1977): 873-89. Reprinted in Pearce (1981), 99-123.

Wood, Michael. "Rocketing to the Apocalypse." Review of *Gravity's Rainbow. New York Review of Books,* 22 March 1973, 22-23.

———. "The Apprenticeship of Thomas Pynchon." Review of *Slow Learner. New York Times Book Review,* 15 April 1984, 1, 28-29.

Wood, Percy. "Sophisticated Sage of Benny Profane." Review of *V. Chicago Tribune Magazine of Books,* 14 April 1963, 4.

Woodward, Kathleen. "Cybernetic Modeling in Recent American Writing: A Critique." *North Dakota Quarterly* 51, no. 1 (Winter 1983): 57-73.

Workman, Mark E. "The Role of Mythology in Modern Literature." *Journal of the Folklore Institute* 18, no. 1 (1981): 35-48.

———. *"Gravity's Rainbow:* A Folkloristic Reading." *Pynchon Notes* 12 (June 1983): 16-25.

Yardley, Jonathan. "The Apprenticeship of Thomas Pynchon." Review of *Slow Learner. Book World,* 22 April 1984, 3.

Young, James Dean. "The Enigma Variations of Thomas Pynchon." *Critique* 10, no. 1 (1967): 69-77.

Zadworna-Fjellestad, Danuta. *"Alice's Adventures in Wonderland" and "Gravity's Rainbow": A Study in Duplex Fiction.* Stockholm: Almqvist and Wiksell, 1986.

Zamora, Lois Parkinson. "The Entropic End: Science and Eschatology in the Works of Thomas Pynchon." *Science/Technology & The Humanities* 3, no. 1 (Winter 1980): 35-43.

———. " 'Le Chaudron fêlé': The Use of Clichés in Fiction by Manuel Puig, Luis Rafael Sánchez and Thomas Pynchon." In *Proceedings of the Tenth Congress of the International Comparative Literature Association.* Vol. 3: Inter-American Literary Relations, edited by Anna Balakian, et al. New York: Garland, 1985. 148-53.

Zand, Nicole. "Le complot de Thomas Pynchon." Review of *Vente à la criée du lot 49. Le Monde,* 17 September 1987.

Zavardeh, Mas'ud. Review of Hendin's *Vulnerable People* and McConnell's *Four Postwar American Novelists. Studies in the Novel* 12 (Winter 1980): 400-403.

Zencey, Eric. "Some Brief Speculations on the Popularity of Entropy as Metaphor." *North American Review* 271, no. 3 (September 1986): 7-10.

Zverev, A.M. "SSHA: itoge goda—'Moralnoe Parazhenie?' " *Inostrannaya literatara* 5 (1979): 209-14.

G. DISSERTATIONS AND THESES

American and Canadian

Harris, Charles B. "Contemporary American Novelists of the Absurd." Southern Illinois University, 1971.

Detweiler, Robert E. "Violence and Art in Postwar American Literature: A Study of O'Connor, Kosinski, Hawkes and Pynchon." University of Rochester, 1972.

Robinson, David Z. "Unaccommodated Man: The Estranged World in Contemporary American Fiction." Duke University, 1972.

Price, Johnathan Lee. "Black Humor: Form as Manipulation." Stanford University, 1972.

Hoenchen, Susan J. "I Have to Keep the Two Things Separate: Polarity in Women in the Contemporary American Novel." Emory University, 1973, 231 pp.

Plater, William M. "Metamorphosis: An Examination of Communications and Community in Hardt, Beckett and Pynchon." University of Illinois, 1974.

Sperry, Joseph P. "Henry Adams and Thomas Pynchon: The Entropic Movement of Self, Society and Truth." Ohio State University, 1974, 153 pp.

Olderod, Jeannie Wortman. "The Multiple Perspective in Modern Experimental Novels: Eight Examples." University of Nebraska, Lincoln, 1974, 278 pp.

Nash, James W. "Chaos, Structure and Situation in the Novels of Thomas Pynchon." University of Houston, 1974, 175 pp.

Hall, Larry Joe. "The Development of Myth in Post-World War II American Novels." North Texas State University, 1974, 253 pp.

Fraisinger, Randall Roy. "To Move a Wild Laughter in the Throat of Death: An Anatomy of Black Humor." University of Missouri, Columbia, 1975, 256 pp.

Bischoff, Joan. "With Manic Laughter: The Secular Apocalypse in American Novels of the 1960's." Lehigh University, 1975, 345 pp.

1. American and Canadian

Harris, Charles B. "Contemporary American Novelists of the Absurd." Southern Illinois University, 1971.

Golden, Robert E. "Violence and Art in Postwar American Literature: A Study of O'Connor, Kosinski, Hawkes and Pynchon." University of Rochester, 1972.

Robinson, David E. "Unaccommodated Man: The Estranged World in Contemporary American Fiction." Duke University, 1972.

Price, Johnathan Lee. "Black Humor: Form as Manipulation." Stanford University, 1972.

Hoerchner, Susan J. " 'I Have to Keep the Two Things Separate': Polarity in Women in the Contemporary American Novel." Emory University, 1973. 231 pp.

Plater, William M. "Metamorphosis: An Examination of Communications and Community in Barth, Beckett and Pynchon." University of Illinois, 1974.

Sperry, Joseph P. "Henry Adams and Thomas Pynchon: The Entropic Movements of Self, Society and Truth." Ohio State University, 1974. 153 pp.

Gilsdorf, Jeanette Wortman. "The Multiple Perspective in Modern Experimental Novels: Eight Examples." University of Nebraska, Lincoln, 1974. 278 pp.

Nash, James W. "Chaos, Structure and Salvation in the Novels of Thomas Pynchon." University of Houston, 1974. 175 pp.

Hall, Larry Joe. "The Development of Myth in Post-World War II American Novels." North Texas State University, 1974. 253 pp.

Freisinger, Randall Roy. " 'To Move Wild Laughter in the Throat of Death': An Anatomy of Black Humor." University of Missouri-Columbia, 1975. 259 pp.

Bischoff, Joan. "With Manic Laughter: The Secular Apocalypse in American Novels of the 1960's." Lehigh University, 1975. 348 pp.

Steinmetz, Joseph James. "Between Zero and One: A Psychohistoric Reading of Thomas Pynchon's Major Works." University of Wisconsin, Madison, 1975. 336 pp.

Strehle, Susan. "Black Humor in Contemporary American Fiction." University of California, Berkeley, 1975.

Tapp, Gary Wesley. "The Story and the Game: Recent Fiction and the Theology of Play." Emory University, 1975. 258 pp.

McNall, Sally Allen. "Order as Surprise: A Stylisic Comparison of Experimental Fiction." Arizona State University, 1975. 206 pp.

Westervelt, Linda Alleyne. "The Role of the Reader in the Modern Anatomy: A Study of the Fiction of John Barth, Robert Coover, and Thomas Pynchon." Rice University, 1976. 219 pp.

Calhoun, John Cadwell. "A Groatsworth of Wit: Parallels in John Barth's *The Sot-Weed Factor* and Thomas Pynchon's *V.*" University of Arkansas, 1976. 616 pp.

Peacock, Allen H., III. "Pynchon's Progress: Slothrop's Errand into the Zone." Senior Honors Thesis, Harvard University, 1976.

Schaub, Thomas Hill. "The Ambiguity of Pynchon's Fact and Fiction." University of Iowa, 1976. 233 pp.

Grant, James Kerr. "The Embroidered Mantle: Order and the Individual in the Fiction of Thomas Pynchon." University of Virginia, 1976. 264 pp.

Siegel, Mark Richard. "Creative Paranoia: Pynchon's Accomplishments in *Gravity's Rainbow.*" University of Arizona, 1976. 284 pp.

Cowart, David Guyland. "Thomas Pynchon's Art of Allusion." Rutgers University, 1977. 284 pp.

Zamora, Lois Parkinson. "The Apocalyptic Vision in Contemporary American Fiction: Gabriel García Márquez, Thomas Pynchon, Julio Cortázar, and John Barth." University of California, Berkeley, 1977. 314 pp.

Schneider, Suzanne Peterson. "Irrealism in Contemporary Literature: A Study of Borges, Barth, and Pynchon." University of Colorado, Boulder, 1977. 187 pp.

Banning, Charles Leslie. "The Time of Our Time: William Gaddis, John Hawkes and Thomas Pynchon." State University of New York, Buffalo, 1977. 180 pp.

Edelstein, Arthur. "Realism and Beyond: Essays on Twentieth-Century Fiction." Stanford University, 1977. 282 pp.

Galicia, Gregory Stephen. "Patterns of Experience: The Participatory Voice in Criticism and Metafiction." Northern Illinois University, 1977. 260 pp.

Porush, David Hillel. "Apocalypses of the Sixties: A Study of the Morphology of a Literary Genre." State University of New York, Buffalo, 1977. 293 pp.

Leder, Mark Randall. "The Use and Theory of Metaphor in the Works of Thomas Pynchon." Yale University, 1977. 329 pp.

Murphy, Earl Paulus. "Thomas Pynchon's *V.*: A Psycho-Structural Study." Saint Louis University, 1977. 137 pp.

Rice-Sayre, Laura Prindle. "Abra-Cadaver: The Anti-Detective Story in Postmodern Fiction." University of Washington, 1977.

Doyle, Linda S. "A Study of Time in Three Novels: *Under the Volcano, One Hundred Years of Solitude,* and *Gravity's Rainbow.*" University of Notre Dame, 1978. 178 pp.

Scheffler, Judith Ann. "The Ultracharacter in Post-World War II American Fiction: A Study of Abstract Characterization in Major Novels of the Period." University of Pennsylvania, 1978. 318 pp.

Krafft, John Monroe. "Historical Imagination in the Novels of Thomas Pynchon." State University of New York, Buffalo, 1978. 406 pp.

Solberg, Sara Margaret. "Resonance: Joyce's *Ulysses* and Pynchon's *V.*" Columbia University, 1978. 418 pp.

McLester-Greenfield, Owana Kaye. "When Even the Best Is Bad: Thomas Pynchon's Alternative to the Wasteland." Drake University, 1978. 450 pp.

Stonehill, Brian. "Art Displaying Art: Self-Consciousness in Novels of Joyce, Nabokov, Gaddis, and Pynchon." University of Chicago, 1978.

Jobson, Christine G. "Thomas Pynchon: Connoisseur of Chaos." Master's Thesis, San Francisco State, 1978.

Weisenburger, Steven Carl. "Accelerated Grimace: American Fiction in the Age of Speed." University of Washington, 1978. 302 pp.

Neralich, Robert John. "Secularization and Secularism in the Works of Gabriel Vahanian, Harvey Cox, Joseph Heller, and Thomas Pynchon." Arkansas University, 1978.

Del Col, Jeffrey Anthony. "Early Clues for the New Direction? The Technocratic Myth in Pynchon and Pirsig." West Virginia University, 1978. 188 pp.

Cooper, Peter Lee. "An Ominous Logic: Thomas Pynchon and Contemporary American Fiction." University of California, Los Angeles, 1978. 453 pp.

Herzberg, Bruce I. "Illusions of Control: A Reading of *Gravity's Rainbow.*" Rutgers University, 1978. 189 pp.

Maddox, Daniel Thomas. "Rocket Blues: Knowledge and Morality in *Gravity's Rainbow.*" American University, 1978.

Price, Ruby Victoria. "Christian Allusions in the Novels of Thomas Pynchon." Rice University, 1979. 372 pp.

Thompson, Gary Lee. "Fictive Models: Carlyle's *Sartor Resartus,* Melville's *The Confidence-Man,* Gaddis' *The Recognitions,* and Pynchon's *Gravity's Rainbow.*" Rice University, 1979. 409 pp.

Davis, Susan Elizabeth Hendricks. "A Counterforce of Readers: The Rhetoric of Thomas Pynchon's Narrative Technique." University of Michigan, 1979. 225 pp.

Katz, Bruce Leslie. "This Ruinous Garden: Readable Signs in Pynchon's *Gravity's Rainbow* with Remarks on Barth's *Giles Goat-Boy.*" Rutgers University, 1979. 347 pp.

Taylor, Patricia Simmons. "Make It New: *Gravity's Rainbow* as Romantic Discovery." University of California, Los Angeles, 1979. 214 pp.

Simmon, Scott Allan. "The *Ulysses* Tradition: Open and Closed Form in the Novels of James Joyce, William Gaddis, and Thomas Pynchon."

University of California, 1979. 341 pp.

Braha, Elliot. "Menippean Form in *Gravity's Rainbow* and in Other Contemporary American Texts." Columbia University, 1979. 242 pp.

Hariman, Robert Donald. "The Public Temper of *Gravity's Rainbow.*" University of Minnesota, 1979. 222 pp.

Huwiler, David Dean. "The Spirit of Play in Recent American Literature." University of California, Davis, 1979. 190 pp.

Mailloux, Peter Alden. "Paradigms Lost: Studies in Non-Cooperation in the Twentieth Century Novel." University of California, Berkeley, 1979. 247 pp.

Black, Joel Dana. "The Second Fall: The Laws of Digression and Gravitation in Romantic Narrative and Their Impact on Contemporary Encyclopaedic Literature." Stanford University, 1979. 383 pp.

Bass, Thomas Alden. "Fiction and History: Essays on the Novels of Flaubert, García Márquez, Coover, and Pynchon." University of Pennsylvania, 1980. 255 pp.

Bisset, David Lee. "Contrary Identities: Subject and Text in Modern Introspective Fiction." University of Virginia, 1980. 769 pp.

Clark, Beverly Lyon. "The Mirror Worlds of Carroll, Nabokov, and Pynchon: Fantasy in the 1860's and 1960's." Brown University, 1980. 429 pp.

Cramer, Carmen Kay. "The New Democratic Protagonist: American Novels and Women Main Characters, 1960-1966." Texas Christian University, 1980. 220 pp.

Guzlowski, John Zbigniew. "The Assault on Character in the Novels of Thomas Pynchon, John Barth, John Hawkes, and William Gaddis." Purdue University, 1980. 221 pp.

Jannone, Claudia Jo. "Sterne, Joyce and Pynchon: World Enough and Words." University of South Florida, 1980. 187 pp.

Bobo, S. C. "Systematic Inanimateness: The Problem of Meaning in Pynchon's *V.*" Master's Thesis, Mississippi State University, 1980.

Krause, V. E. *"Gravity's Rainbow:* A Study in Narration and Reader Response." Master's Thesis, University of Texas, Austin, 1980.

Larsson, Donald Foss. "The Film Breaks: Thomas Pynchon and the Cinema." University of Wisconsin, Madison, 1980. 337 pp.

Mazurek, Raymond Allen. "The Fiction of History: The Presentation of History in Recent American Literature." Purdue University, 1980. 253 pp.

Munley, Ellen Wojdak. "Caught in the Act: Naming the Novels of Thomas Pynchon and Nathalie Sarraute." Boston College, 1980. 199 pp.

Werner, Craig Hansen. "Paradoxical Resolutions: James Joyce and Contemporary American Fiction." University of Illinois, Urbana-Champaign, 1980. 313 pp.

Young, Thomas Earl. "Mirror, Mirror: Dimensions of Reflexivity in Post-Modern British and American Fiction." Michigan State University, 1980. 317 pp.

Hite, Molly. "Ideas of Order in the Novels of Thomas Pynchon." University of Washington, 1981. 265 pp.

Crowell, Douglas Edward. " 'When You See Someone's Head Entirely Bandaged, You Know He Is Evil': Reading *Miss Lonelyhearts, The Dead Father, Lost in the Funhouse,* and *Gravity's Rainbow.*" State University of New York, Buffalo, 1981. 207 pp.

Cullen, Robert Joseph. "Words and a Yarn: Language and Narrative Technique in the Works of Thomas Pynchon." University of California, Los Angeles, 1981. 222 pp.

Hindin, Beverly Narod. "Death and the Imaginative Vision of Modern and Post-Modern American Fiction." University of Pennsylvania, 1981. 255 pp.

Limon, John Keith. "Imagining Science: The Influence and Metamorphosis of Science in Charles Brockden Brown, Edgar Allan Poe, and Nathaniel Hawthorne." University of California, Berkeley, 1981. 460 pp.

Palmeri, Frank Anthony. "The Short Menippean Narrative, with Particular Reference to Swift's *A Tale of a Tub,* Melville's *The Confidence-Man,* and Pynchon's *The Crying of Lot 49.* Columbia University, 1981. 255 pp.

148

Gorman, Lawrence John. *"Gravity's Rainbow:* The Promise and Trap of Mythology." Northern Illinois University, 1981. 262 pp.

Olster, Stacey Michelle. "Subjective Historicism in the Post-Modern American Novel: A Study of Norman Mailer, Thomas Pynchon, and John Barth." University of Michigan, 1981. 393 pp.

Watkins, Leah Helen. "Exploring the Interface: Post-Modernism and Changing Notions of Literature." University of Michigan, 1981. 189 pp.

Hill, Robert Ratcliff. "Epistemological Dilemmas in the Works of Norman Mailer and Thomas Pynchon: The Themes and Motifs of Systemization, Paranoia, and Entropy." University of Tulsa, 1982. 309 pp.

Lattimer, Lois J. "Parallel Themes of Franz Kafka and Thomas Pynchon." Master's Thesis. Florida Atlantic University, 1982. 79 pp.

Morris, Paul. "Beyond the Zero: *Gravity's Rainbow* and Modern Critical Theory." City University of New York, 1982. 460 pp.

Oxley, Robert Morris. "Lists in Literature: Homer, Whitman, Joyce, Borges." University of Wisconsin, Madison, 1982. 261 pp.

Papadokos, Juliet. "Reality and the Journey to Knowledge in the Novels of Thomas Pynchon." State University of New York, Stony Brook, 1982. 290 pp.

Bacchilega, Christina. "Palimpsest Readings: The Marchen and Contemporary Fiction." State University of New York, Binghamton, 1983. 242 pp.

Comnes, Judith Chambers. *"Gravity's Rainbow* as Hermeneutic Text." University of South Florida, 1983. 270 pp.

Tourtelott, James Elliott. "In the Realm of Dominus Blicero: A Reading of *Gravity's Rainbow."* State University of New York, Stony Brook, 1983. 329 pp.

Daw, Frederick J. L. "Us and Them: Technological Hierarchies in Fowles and Pynchon." University of Western Ontario, 1983.

Brashears de Gonzàles, Ann. " 'La Novela Totalizadora': Pynchon's *Gravity's Rainbow* and Fuentes' *Terra Nostra."* University of South Carolina, 1983. 201 pp.

MacLaine, Donald Brenton. "Absent-Centred Structure in Five Modern Novels: Henry James' *The Princess Casamassima,* Joseph Conrad's *The Secret Agent,* Andrei Bely's *Petersberg,* Joseph Heller's *Catch-22,* and Thomas Pynchon's *Gravity's Rainbow.*" University of British Columbia, 1983.

Worley, Joan Yvonne. " 'Film into Fiction': Thomas Pynchon and Manuel Puig." Ohio University, 1983. 195 pp.

Kim, Seong Kon. "Journey into the Past: The Historical and Mythical Imagination of Barth and Pynchon." State University of New York, Buffalo, 1984. 228 pp.

Ingraham, Catherine T. "Complexion and Complexity: Thomas Pynchon's Reading of the American Scene." Johns Hopkins University, 1984. 220 pp.

Freeman, Christine. "Speaking the Silent Mutiny of the Muted: Narrative Heresy in Fuentes' *Terra Nostra* and Pynchon's *Gravity's Rainbow.*" Kent State University, 1984. 262 pp.

Verschueren, Walter Pierre. "Literature and Repetition: The Case of American Postmodernism." State University of New York, Binghamton, 1984. 210 pp.

Jones, Dale Wayne. "Aesthetics of Apocalypse: A Study of the Grotesque Novel in America." University of Wisconsin, Madison, 1984. 209 pp.

Cornell, M. Doretta. "Myths against the Void: Mythmaking in Twentieth Century Literature (T.S. Eliot, Wallace Stevens, and Thomas Pynchon)." University of Missouri, Columbia, 1984. 256 pp.

Tylee, Claire M. "The Early Short Fiction of Thomas Pynchon." Master's Thesis. University of Málaga, Spain, 1984.

Bayerl, Elizabeth Ann. "Tangled Hierarchies: *Godel, Escher, Bach: An Eternal Golden Braid* and *Gravity's Rainbow.*" Syracuse University, 1985. 305 pp.

Zencey, Eric. "Entropy as Root Metaphor." Claremont Graduate School, 1986. 320 pp.

Sublett, Bruce L. "Archetypes and Patterns of the Grail Romance in Thomas Pynchon's *Gravity's Rainbow.*" Master's Thesis. Stephen F.

Austin State University, 1986. 107 pp.

Toia, Elaine M. "Thomas Pynchon's *V.:* A Curious Landscape." Lehigh University, 1986. 166 pp.

Horvath, Brooke K. "Dropping Out: Spiritual Crisis and Countercultural Attitudes in Four American Novelists of the 1960's." Purdue University, 1986. 158 pp.

Campbell, Elizabeth A. "Disposable Containers: Metonymy in the Novel." University of Virginia, 1983. 264 pp.

Price, Penelope. "*Gravity's Rainbow:* Thomas Pynchon's Use of the Media." Arizona State University, 1985. 146 pp.

Kharpertian, Theodore D. " 'A Hand to Turn the Time': Mennipean Satire and the Postmodernist American Fiction of Thomas Pynchon." McGill University, 1985.

Smetak, Jacqueline R. "Essays on the Fiction of Thomas Pynchon." University of Iowa, 1986. 334 pp.

Stevenson, Sheryl Ann. "The Never-Last Word: Parody, Ideology, and the Open Work." University of Maryland, 1986. 246 pp.

Dewey, Joseph Owen. "In a Dark time: The Apocalyptic Temper of American Literature in the Atomic Age." Purdue University, 1986. 336 pp.

Jessee, Sharon Adele. "A Monotony of Fine Weather: Imagined Worlds in Contemporary American Fiction." University of Tulsa, 1986.

Kowalewski, Michael. "Violence and Verbal Form in American Fiction." Rutgers University, 1986.

Olsen, Lance. "Nameless Things and Thingless Names: An Essay on Postmodern Fantasy." University of Virginia, 1986.

Sapanaro, Richard G. "Post-Industrial Society and Post-Modern Literature: A Systems Approach to *Gravity's Rainbow*." University of California, Irvine, 1986. 279 pp.

LaPointe, Adriane. " 'Is It Okay to Be a Luddite?': Mechanism in the Fiction of Dickens and Pynchon." University of Chicago, 1986. 204 pp.

151

McLaughlin, Robert. "Supernatural Other Worlds and Spiritual Afterlife in Thomas Pynchon's *Gravity's Rainbow.*" Fordham University, 1987. 330 pp.

Frost, Janice W. " 'Overcoming the Tradition': A Social Constructionist Approach to *V., The Crying of Lot 49,* and *Gravity's Rainbow.*" University of Utah, 1987. 343 pp.

Burda, Helen E. "Redemption in the Novels of John Barth, John Hawkes, and Thomas Pynchon: 'By indirections find directions out' (*Hamlet* II.i.66)." Indiana University of Pennsylvania, 1987. 271 pp.

Campbell, Gregor Duncan. "Historical Consciousness in the Fiction of William Gaddis, Thomas Pynchon, and Robert Coover: A Reading of *The Recognitions, Gravity's Rainbow,* and *The Public Burning.*" University of Toronto, 1988. 426 pp.

Tabbi, Joseph. "The Psychology of Machines: Technology and Personal Identity in the Work of Norman Mailer and Thomas Pynchon." University of Toronto, 1989. 215 pp.

2. British

Tate, Miss C. L. "Parody: An Aspect of Literary Self-Consciousness in Contemporary American Fiction with Particular Reference to Barth, Mailer and Pynchon." London, U.C., 1976.

Cross, Miss M. J. "The Presentation of Self in Contemporary American Literature with Special Reference to the Work of Charles Olson, Frank O'Hara, William Burroughs and Thomas Pynchon." Nottingham, 1976.

Cooper, M. J. "Centres and Boundaries: The Presentation of Self in the Work of William Burroughs, Thomas Pynchon, Charles Olson and Robert Duncan." Nottingham, 1977. 377 pp.

Mackenzie, Ursula A. "The Reaction against Social Realism in Post-War American Fiction Concentrating on Nabokov, Mailer, Barth and Pynchon." Nottingham, 1978. 444 pp.

Bruce, Gina. "Consciousness in Modern American and English Novels: Golding, Durrell, Fowles, Purdy, Pynchon, Barth." Nottingham, 1982.

Dawson, G. P. "The Dilemma of Contemporary Existence in the Fiction of Thomas Pynchon." Nottingham, 1984. 288 pp.

Lyttle, I. "A Reader-Response Approach to Thomas Pynchon's Fiction." Belfast, 1984.

Marriott, A. D. "Thomas Pynchon." Manchester, 1984.

Dugdale, J. V. "A Study of Pynchon." Cambridge, Trinity, 1986.

Appendix

Pynchon's Juvenilia

Purple and Gold

Vol. IX, No. 2   OYSTER BAY, N. Y., NOVEMBER 13, 1952   Fifteen Cents

SENIOR CLASS CAST TO PRESENT "YOU CAN'T TAKE IT WITH YOU"

If you happen to be inquisitive enough to peek into the auditorium after school to see what all the ruckus is about, you'll find it's probably an over loud prompter, a Senior thespian putting a bit of emotion into his acting, or Mr. Grady giving some constructive criticism. If you're a teacher, you'll probably shake your head and mutter, "It happens every year." If you're a student, though, you'll probably perk up your ears or do a double take, because this year's Senior Play is one of the wackiest to come along in a long time.

It's called "YOU CAN'T TAKE IT WITH YOU," by George S. Kaufman and Moss Hart and is classed (and rightly so), a comedy. It concerns the antics of a slightly eccentric family and the clash that results when it meets the outside world. The Sycamore brood live just around the corner from Columbia University in New York, and under Grandpa, the benevolent old patriarch of the family, who spends his time evading the Income Tax, going to zoos and commencements, and collecting snakes, they pursue these various activities, rugged individualists all, without giving a hoot about anyone else. Penny writes plays, Essie makes candy and is an inspiring ballerina, Paul and De Pinna manufacture fireworks, Ed plays the marimba, prints, and makes masks. There is also Kolenkhov the ballet instructor, a boorish Russian.

Well, it seems that Alice Sycamore, about the only normal member of the family, falls in love with her boss's son, Anthony Kirby, Jr. Kirby, Sr., is a big Wall Street tycoon, and his wife is a prominent socialite.

Penny plans a party for them, and Alice—justly apprehensive—has arranged for them to act as normal as the Sycamores can get in the Kirby's presence. Then, the night before they are scheduled to come, the Kirbys accidentally (although later we discover Tony planned it purposely) drop in in the midst of a typical night at the Sycamores, which, unfortunately, does not exactly coincide with the Kirbys' idea of a typical evening. Alice, of course, is horrified, and then to top it off, the Department of Justice stages a raid on the Sycamore household. It seems that Ed, in selling the candies Essie makes, has quite unintentionally included Marxist doctrine instead of advertising matter. Everyone, including the Kirbys, is hustled off to jail. However, the story ends happily. Alice gets Tony, and—but you'll have to see it to find out how all this comes about.

Starred in the cast are Jim George as Grandpa Vanderhof, Norma Sprague as Alice, Dan Smolnik as Tony Kirby, Bob

Chorus Plans Yule Program

The members of the Oyster Bay High School Chorus have been progressing very rapidly with their plans for the Christmas program. They have selected some very beautiful arrangements.

A number of students are also planning to attend the "All Long Island Festival." They are very proud to have fulfilled the requirements and are certainly looking forward to this event.

The members of the Girls' Glee Club have also been working very diligently, but at the same time they have been enjoying their work with Mr. Aebischer.

Mr. Aebischer has also organized a male quartet and "The Harmonettes," whose leader is Dorothea Custis. At the present time he is finding the results very promising.

Weltmann as De Pinna, Herman Lowman as Paul Sycamore, Mary Alice Fedosoff as Essie, John Nostrand as Ed, Charles Rothmann and June Crawford as Mr. and Mrs. Kirby, Peggy Disbrow as Penny, and Gary Elsner as Kolenkhov. Also featured are Antoinette Telegri, Arnold Engelstein, Marilin Olsen, Henry Bester, Sam Bozzello, Frances James Gil Herbert and Denise Warren.

Besides the cast and its busy rehearsals, there are the many committees connected with the Senior Play. The Publicity Committee and the Business Staff, headed by Tony Kohm and Mrs. Manser, are hard at work with ticket sales, posters, news releases, and boosters. The stage crew, headed by Bob Myrato, has been busy hammering together, painting, and setting up scenery, performing a vital function in any stage production. The Props Committee, head ed by Ruth McComie, faces something akin to a fantastical scavenger hunt, having to procure such items as a stuffed crocodile, a Roman toga, and a marimba.

And through the scene of bustle and hard work runs that tense undercurrent of excitement which attends any play production. As the big night approaches, members of the cast practice cues and lines, polish their speeches and interpretations, and practice their stage movements.

The Senior Play of 1952 will be held Friday evening, November 14, in the High School Auditorium. Tickets are eighty cents. At 8:15 the curtain will rise on what the Class of '53 hopes will be one of the most successful Senior Plays ever produced. You can help it be this, by your attendance.

November:

13—First Report Cards.
13—Senior Play.
14—Assembly.
15—Bayshore at home.
21—G. O. Football Hop.
26-28—Thanksgiving Vacation.
29—Basketball game at Sewanhaka.

December:

2—Basketball game at St. Dominic's.
4—Senior Party.
5—Honor Society Installation.
6—Basketball game at Long Beach.
9—Conservatory Players Assembly.
12—Basketball game at home with Sewanhaka.

Sock Hop Successful

On October 24, nearly 400 teen-agers from St. Dominic's and Oyster Bay High Schools, in addition to many who had been graduated during the past severn' years, danced in their socks to the strains of the "Victorians." The "Sock Hop," according to reports from the students and the custodians, drew the largest and most orderly crowd ever to attend a dance at the high school.

In addition, Teen-Age Club membership swelled to 417. This makes the club an unusual and outstanding teen-age organization.

Entertainment was furnished by the guests themselves, organized by the T-A Club. The "Harmoniers," consisting of Johnny Foster, Zeke Barrum, Gil Herbert, Lawrence Giles, James Davis, Norman Wilson and Robert Pickney, sang "Dearest" and a modern rendition of "Old MacDonald." Bernard Murphy gave a wonderful imitation of Johnny Ray singing "Cry." Gil Herbert and Norman Wilson did some fancy dance steps. The "Victorians," with Fred James on drums, Victor Maffei on accordion and Bob Maffei on guitar, provided the music.

Gladys Hornosky

HONOR SOCIETY PLANS INDUCTION

The officers of the Honour Society for the ensuing year are: John Nostrand, president; Bob White, man, vice-president; Janice George, secretary; and Peggy Disbrow, treasurer.

The first meeting of the Honor Society was held on October 16 during the noon hour. At that meeting plans were made for the induction of new members to be held early in December. At this time five per cent of the senior class and five per cent of the junior class will be admitted to membership in the Oyster Bay chapter of the National Honor Society at

Oyster Bay Upsets Westbury H.S., 13-12

On November 1, Oyster Bay, undermanned, out-weighted and out-reached Westbury team, fought a heavily favored Westbury team, and beat the 13-12. Coming from behind twice our boys turned the tables on Westbury, which has a reputation for being a tough team, and gave them some of their own medicine. Westbury's touchdown in the first quarter resulted from a very lucky "break." We were penalized 50 yards for excessive roughness which put the ball on our one-yard line. Our boys put up a magnificent goal line stand, but Alexander finally plunged over for the touchdown on the fourth down. Alexander then missed the placement for the extra point, and the score was 6-0.

After several punt exchanges and short drives by each side, we took possession of the ball late the second period on Westbury's 45-yard line. McNamara hit McDax with a long pass on the 2. Carl bucked for five more yards and with only seconds remaining Robinson scored on the "Statue of Liberty" play around his own end. The attempted run for the extra point was stopped.

During the third period each side gained possession of the ball several times but made little or no yardage. This same type of play continued for the first seven minutes in the last quarter when Westbury drove to our 14-yard line on several short runs. They finally scored on a pass play which was nearly stopped when the receiver was hit but not brought

(Continued on Page Five)

G. O. PLANS

The G. O., busy as usual, has held two meetings since the last issue of the P. & G. went to press. The first was held September 30, 1952; at this meeting the class representatives were given subscription blanks for the P. & G. Subscription sales were quite gratifying this year.

The second meeting was held October 30, and Mike Fensel began the meeting with a talk about the Red Cross. There will be a drive from November 13 to 18. Let's all get behind this most worthy cause. When your G. O. representative asks you to give, do be willingly and as generously as possible.

Sam Bozzello presented plans for the show case and from what I've seen of them, it's a pretty sharp affair—the perfect thing to show off the many trophies won by our championship teams. The case will replace the bulletin board in the main hall, so keep your eyes open for it. We hope to get it before Christmas.

Bethpage has extended the G. O. a cordial invitation to attend one of their meetings and give them some information about the manner in which we conduct our meetings. Two of our representatives are going.

The G. O., in order to promote capacity voting, is extending baby sitting aid to the local polling places. This is another example of the fine work done by this year's G. O. Dotty Platt and Jean Diedrich were at the Bayville polls; Monica Rumpf and Priscilla Frank, Syosset; June Hemrich and June Crawford, East Norwich; and Oyster Bay was covered by Carla Hubbard, Lucille Iannicello, Judy Mills, Virginia Furman, Edith Kraft and Peggy Disbrow.

Well, that's about all for this issue, but don't forget to support your G. O. every time you get a chance. It's working for you, so you work for it.

Seniors

There hasn't been much recent news of events from the other schools, but from St. Dominic's came a poem I think you'll enjoy.

"Seniors"

The year we've been waiting for,
Is now fast slipping by,
We seniors are dignified
As freshman look and sigh.
They long for—as we did once,
The title once esteemed.
It now belongs to you know.
The goal of which we've dreamed.
I'll bet every one of the seniors
can look back and remember when
they thought, "Just wait'l I'M a
senior . . ."

an assembly of the entire student body.

G. M. Pulis Stars At Band Concert

Since the last edition of the P. & G., the High School Band has given two concerts. On Oct. 19 sponsored by the Quentin Roosevelt Post, No. 4, of the American Legion, the Band traveled to Kings Park, where it presented a hour-long concert. On Monday, Nov. 3rd, at its Fall Concert, the Band featured a cornet trio which played "Trifolium" by Leidzen, its flute section, which presented "Meditation" from "Thais" by Massanet; and its twirling corps which twirled lighted batons to the music of "Indiana State Band" by Farrar. The guest artist, Gardon M. Pulis, first trombonist of the New York Philharmonic Symphony Orchestra, presented a group of trombone solos during the second part of the program.

On Nov. 21 and 22, several band members will attend the All-State Festival to be held at Amityville. There they will participate in a band composed of outstanding instrumentalists from Nassau and Suffolk counties. The annual Christmas Concert will be presented during the last week of school prior to the Christmas vacation.

Purple and Gold, 13 November 1952, 2.

"The Voice of the Hamster"

Dear Sam,

You may remember me—I don't know. I met you at that party in Huntington last August. I was the squat individual with the red crewcut who was
doing the imitation of Winston Churchill. Anyway, you expressed interest
in this school I go to and asked me to get in touch with you. So, here I am.

Hamster High is located on a rock about a half mile off the South Shore,
and not a very big rock at that, as anybody can tell you who's been there at
high tide. Nobody seems to know why they call the place Hamster High,
other than the highly debatable rumor that its founder, J. Fattington Woodgrouse, had a strong liking for the fuddy little creatures. There is a statue of
J. Fattington Woodgrouse in front of the school. He is a little bald-headed
man with a pot belly, and he looks like a cross between the last Martian and
a hungry barracuda. Last Hallowe'en someone wrote on this statue a very
nasty word in bright orange paint. There was a big scandal. I was suspended
for four weeks.

Maybe the fact that we're fairly well isolated accounts for why Hamster
High is—well, not exactly crazy, but—slightly odd. Take for example our
trig techer, Mr. Faggiaducci. He's a quiet respectable young man who
wears thick glasses with chartreuse rims. He also wears peg pants, satin
shirt, cool cardigan, and bop beret. He tears around in a long, baby-blue
hotrod sedan, and he's always telling be-bop jokes in class. There's nothing
actually wrong with him, it's just that he used to be a bop drummer, and now
he wishes he were back with the boys at Birdland and Eddie Condon's. He
talks to himself a lot and I've heard rumors he takes heroin. A real "gone
guy."

Then of course there's our principal, Mr. Sowfurkle. This boy also has
music leanings—he plays the bagpipes. The bad thing about it is that he uses
school hours to practice. He's very devoted to the bloody instrument. He
locks himself in his office for about an hour every day to play it. Somehow
one gets the idea he doesn't like interruptions. He was born in the hills of
Tennessee, and he still carries a shotgun with him, a nasty thing with a
sawed-off barrel. Anyway, one day the chemistry teacher somehow
wandered into his inner sanctum and started banging on the door, and old
Furk got real excited. Poor Miss Phipps. We had to get a new door, too.

You might think we're pretty limited as far as sports go, being out on a
rock like we are, but that isn't so. Of course, we can't have our own football
or baseball fields, so we use the ones in the nearest town, Riverhampton. I
feel sorry for Coach Willis. He turned down a chance to coach Football at
one of the Big Ten colleges and came to Hamster High instead. Coach
Willis drinks a lot.

He smokes like a fiend, too, so that the Alumni Association is screaming to fire him for setting a bad example for the boys. Coach Willis claims that it's the teams that have driven him to drink. He says: "What can you do with a football team that consistently runs the wrong way, a basketball team which refuses to dribble the ball, and a track team which is afraid to high jump, and throws the shot-put underhand?" In a way, I think he's right, about football at least. In the past three years we've lost every game except one, and that was a tie with some grade school. The only reason we were able to tie them was because the grade school team was continually being penalized for unnecessary roughness.

But still the crowds come out and cheer for our boys, so colorful and manly-looking in their brown fur football uniforms, and they cheer our loyal little team mascot, Talleyrand the Hamster. We keep Tallyrand muzzled and on a long leash, for he is a vicious little monster. This hamster has razor sharp fangs which must be at least an inch long. If you don't believe me, I can show you the scars where Tallyrand autographed my wrist.

But now I must say so long because I am getting tired, and I have a lot of trig homework to do. Not that it *has* to be done for tomorrow, as chances are Mr. Faggiaducci won't be there; he's out on another binge. Remind me sometime to tell you about the time the State Education Inspector came to Hamster High. Poor fellow—he's in an institution now. And remember me to Beer-belly MacPherson and the rest of the mob.

Your drunken amigo,
Boscoe Stein.

* * *

Purple and Gold, 18 December 1952, 3

"Voice of the Hamster"

Dear Sam,

In your last letter you mentioned that you wanted to hear about the time the State Education Inspector came to Hamster High. Well, it was sort of ironic since the grandfather, J. Fattington Woodgrouse, founded our school. This guy was little and fat, like the original, and he wore a stupid-looking pork-pie hat. Mr. Sowfurkle greeted him warmly and proceeded to take him on a tour of the school.

It seems the first class he went to was Miss Phipps' chemistry class. I don't take chemistry myself, but I got this straight from Sid Scully, who is at present engaged in an exhaustive study of the physiological effects of complex nicotine compounds upon the human body. He is also a chain smoker. Anyway, Crazy Harrigan was doing some work in the lab with unstable plutonium isotopes. You remember Crazy—the guy who blew up the Farmingdale Bank. Just as Mr. Woodgrouse opened the lab door, out tore Crazy, yelling at the top of his lungs, and he cannonballed into the inspector. It's a good thing he knocked the inspector down because a minute later there was a terrific explosion from inside the lab, and half the wall came down on him. Crazy had got away down the hall, and it seemed that Mr. Woodgrouse was the only casualty. He took him down to the infirmary and patched him up.

Then all through the day, little accidents kept happening to him. It's fantastic, but it always happens when somebody we don't want comes wandering around. He saw more of the infirmary than anything else. First, in Mr. McGinty's physics class, a ten-pound weight rolled off the desk and hit him on the foot. Then in the cafeteria someone bumped him and knocked his meal all over his new Brooks Brothers suit, ruining it quite permanently. Around the first period he mistook the door to the dumbwaiter shaft for the men's room and took a quick trip from the third floor to the cellar the hard way. He was in pretty bad shape when we found him, so we took him down to the infirmary. Then he wandered into Mr. Faggiaducci's class while Mr. Faggiaducci was giving us an exhibition of bop drumming. Mr. Faggiaducci's hand slipped. The inspector looked awful funny with that drumstick halfway down his throat. After that, he wandered out onto the archery course, which was a mistake in the first place, since we had loudspeakers warning people that Crazy Harrigan's archery team was practicing. I pity the U. S. Army when those guys get drafted. Let Crazy even see any kind of a lethal weapon and he goes "nuts." I guess that Mr. Woodgrouse couldn't hear the warnings through the bandages on his head. A rescue party arrived just in time to see him being pursued by a band of madmen, an arrow through his pork-pie hat and another in his shoulder. We took him down to the infirmary again.

He would have left then, but Coach Willis wanted him to watch football practice. Everything went O.K. until Coach Willis caught wind of the fact that Mr. Woodgrouse had played collegiate football. Before the poor inspector knew what was happening, he was in the quarterback position, the ball had been snapped, and he was watching eleven stalwart specimens of American manhood charging at him with blood in their eyes. I think he had one last fleeting moment of sanity before they hit him, and then he went down beneath a mountain of brown fur football uniforms. And to top it all, Talleyrand the Hamster got loose and bit him. We dragged him down again to the infirmary and fixed up the wound—which required two stiches—and the other injuries he had acquired. I think there was also a couple of vertebrae misplaced.

He went away quite peacefully with the men in the white coats; they didn't even need a straitjacket for him. He was talking happily to himself and laughing. He was singing a little song, too: "First the wall fell, then all the arrows, then the mob in the hamster skins, then that (here he said a very uncouth word) bit me but I don't care. They set off an atom bomb on me, they dropped things on my feet, they rammed things down my throat, but I'm still happy. They set booby traps on me but I don't care anymore—hahahahaha!"

Poor guy. Every week Mr. Faggiaducci goes over to see him and cheers him up with a drum rendition. Sometimes I think that Mr. Faggiaducci is—but never mind. They say that Mr. Woodgrouse will be out in another month. He was a good guy really. One sad note: somehow he lost that cute little pork-pie hat.

Well, I guess that's all for this time. Tell me how it's doing at O.B. H. S., will you?

Be seeing you,
Roscoe Stein.

* * *

Purple and Gold, 22 January 1953, 2, 4.

"Voice of the Hamster"

Dear Sam,

Sorry I haven't written sooner, but I'm in the midst of recovering from a party I attended New Year's Eve. It was what can only be called a riot, and that's about what it ended up as. The party was thrown by Sid Scully's sister Marge, and there must have been over a hundred people there. Everything was quiet until Crazy Harrigan, with some mob from Queens, started a conga line sometime around 1:30 in the morning, and that was about all it took to start an argument. Marge objected to the noise, and Sid agreed with her. Sid got pretty mad and started shoving Crazy around, Crazy threw a punch at Sid, Sid threw one back, Crazy hit Sid over the head with the punch bowl, and pandemonium broke loose—before we knew it we had a full scale free-for-all on our hands. Marge was crying, Sid was sitting on the floor clutching his head and swearing a blue streak, and their St. Bernard, O'Malley by name, was gaily romping through the whole mess and wrecking chairs, lamps—anything that happened to be in the way. The men from Queens, evidently suffering from delusions that they were musketeers or some thing, were happily duelling with the curtain rods, with Mr. Scully's imported Oriental drapes as cloaks. Crazy Harrigan was dashing around with a chair like a lion tamer, screaming some nonsense about how he was a jolly good fellow and if anyone denied it Crazy would bash his head in. About that time the men in blue arrived, and we started to calm down a bit—all, that is, except Moe Klonk, who climbed up on a chair and started yelling about how that was capitalistic oppression and bourgeois tyranny, etc. Finally he got acquainted with the business end of a nightstick the hard way, and that sort of put an end to the party. Sid had to have two stitches taken and there were a lot of split lips and bloody noses, and Marge was almost in hysterics. Happy New Year!

In your last letter you said you wanted to know more about Mr. Rafael Faggiaducci, who teaches "trig" at Hamster High. For Christmas our "trig" class gave Mr. Faggiaducci a necktie with an inscription that lights up in the dark. The first day after Christmas vacation, Mr. Faggiaducci came into class with a large red mark across his face, but he refused to tell us what had happened. We also gave him a gold-plated drumstick inscribed "To Coolcat Faggiaducci from the Boys."

The "Boys" (note well the capital B) are a peculiar and very select group. They occupy the rear seats. Officially they are there to learn trigonometry. Actually they are engaged, under the leadership of Crazy Harrigan and Big Bob Woods, in a fascinating experiment in psychology entailing the instilling of paranoid hallucinations into the logical mind by psychoanalytic deletion of the super-ego. In other words, we are trying to see how much Faggiaducci can take before he flips his lid.

And you may be sure we are succeeding, although Faggiaducci does not exactly appreciate this. Already, he screams, his psychologist says he is getting delusions of persecution; that is, he is imagining that there is a conspiracy against him. You know the funny thing about it? There is!

For one thing, Faggiaducci hates the song "High Noon"—he goes "nuts" every time he hears it. So, John Trodsky brings his guitar to class, and we all sing, "Do not forsake me, Faggiaducci," etc. He gets very, very peeved sometimes. I can show you a scar where I was hit by a compass Faggiaducci threw in a blind fit of rage. We also have the habit of laughing unexpectedly. It may be during a test, when the whole room is quiet—all of a sudden there is a huge roar from the back of the room. Every time Faggiaducci jumps as if he had sat on a mousetrap. Sometimes that happens too. We also pulled a real cool bit a few weeks ago. At a prearranged signal, the whole class started rocking from side to side. Faggiaducci said, "Stop that rocking!" and Sid Scully laughed and said, "What rocking?" Faggiaducci got mad and called the principal, Mr. Sowfurkle, and said, "My class is rocking back and forth. Come up and do something about it." So, the inevitable happened; when Furk came into the room, we stopped rocking and sat perfectly still. The conversation which followed between Faggiaducci and the principal I leave to your own imagination.

Well, Sam, I guess that's about all for now. Write soon and tell me if you have any teachers like Faggiaducci at Oyster Bay High.

As always,

Bosc.

* * *

161

Maffei Busy At Hofstra

In this issue I would like to introduce to you, Bob Maffei, an 18-year-old Bayvillite. Some of the "old-timers" in O. B. H. S. will remember Bob because of his friendly manner and his active participation in many school activities.

Bob, who is beginning his freshman year in Hofstra, is taking English, history, business law, accounting, orientation, gym, and R. O. T. C.

Bob regrets that he didn't take algebra in high school. He suggests that a commercial student get a background in math, science, and a language. He also suggests that a student following an academic course in high school take some commercial subjects such as typing, shorthand, or bookkeeping in case he should be unable to complete college and have to work.

In Hofstra there are about 100 clubs to which a student may belong. The language clubs are open to anyone, the Italian Club being most popular because of the many pizza parties.

Bob enjoys ice hockey, soccer, and football. His many hobbies include reading sports magazines, playing the guitar, and working jig-saw puzzles.

When asked his opinion of girls, Bob promptly replied, "If you want to enjoy 'em, don't go near 'em!"

Being a freshman this year, Bob knows the "ins and outs" of the initiation system at Hofstra. Hazing lasted three weeks. At the end of the second week two contests, a tug-of-war and a greased-pole climb, were held between the "green" freshmen and the sophomores. If the freshmen had won both events, hazing would have been discontinued; however, they lost one so hazing went on for another week.

In order to escape getting demerits from an upperclassman, a freshman must wear his beanie, know the alma mater and school fight songs, have matches and pencils for upper classmen, and carry a handbook of the school tradition, school clubs, the alma mater, and the layout of the school. If a student didn't have one of these articles, he would receive a certain number of demerits. The average number of demerits a freshman gets is 40 or 50. Bob, however, got 127.

The real purpose of hazing in Hofstra is to get the student better acquainted with the school, school clubs, school songs, and the upper classmen.

We know that Bob will do as much for Hofstra as he did for Oyster Bay High School.

Nancy George.

The American Campus

There have been many requests for more college information for undedicated seniors. We have finally dug into our Sears-Roebuck catalogue and have come up with a number of the lesser known institutions of learning.

Southeaster North Dakota Agricultural College — Located near Albuquerque, New Mexico, this school has turned out many great sports' stars. You all, I am sure, remember Blanchard and Davis. These two great football players will long be in the minds of every red-blooded American boy. Both Fenwick C. Blanchard and Gasgrove Davis graduated with big honors from S. N. D. A. C.

All of you students majoring in physical education should set your sights on this famous school.

Colorado School of Bean Pickers—This college has much to offer for boys interested in outdoor careers. Small classes with small professors.

Pituitary Tech. — Students interested in medicine will find this wonderful school just what the doctor ordered. Courses include: taxidermy, scalp massage, brain surgery, and body snatching.

Anthracite Shale School of Mines —(Staten Island). For students handy with pick and shovel, here is the place to learn the secrets of coal mining. Upon completing the course the student receives an autographed photograph of John L. Lewis and a union card.

Crankcase College — This well-known engineering school, located at Great Pt, Ohio, has available a great variety of courses. They include: basket weaving, block building, and a specialized postgraduate course in tinker-toy construction. Students must supply their own erector sets and screw drivers.

University of Southern Exposure—An agricultural college of high esteem. Here the young chick-farmer is educated in subjects such as: bootlegging, how to be a successful chicken thief, the raising and house-breeding of Black Widow spiders, and home sandblasting made easy.

There you have a few small but excellent colleges and training schools. For more information send a card to the following address:

Warrick Robinson
Ward 967
Bellevue Hospital
New York
N. Y.

VOICE OF THE HAMSTER

Dear Sam,

Did it! Passed trig! I was taking it half-year, you know, with The Boys, and we finally succeeded in getting Faggiaducci to the point where he was completely fed up with us. He got so mad that the day of the Regents he refused to proctor the exam. So we were stuck with some neurotic Czech who screamed instead of talked.

Anyway, we started singing, "Do not forsake me, Faggiaducci," and he got purple and screamed— screamed, mind you, not yelled— like Faggiaducci—"Shut up or I'll kick you all out!" Then he started swearing and insulting us and throwing things until finally he got us pretty riled. Now you know there's one thing meaner than The Boys, and that's The Boys riled. Sid Scully called the Czech something very uncomplimentary; Crazy Harrigan hit him from behind with a ruler; and Bob Woods tripped him with a chair when he swung at Sid. He headed out of the room, intending to call the principal. That did it! En masse, The Boys arose, surrounded the Czech, picked him up bodily, stuffed him in the dumbwaiter, and left him there until we could finish the exam in peace.

Faggiaducci had said that the best mark he had expected was somewhere in the low 60's; as it was, there was no mark lower than 92. (Don't ask me how we did it!) This, of course, had a severe psychological effect on Faggiaducci. He hasn't been to school in a week. I hear he had a breakdown. The Czech? Well, nobody uses that dumbwaiter shaft anymore, and so we decided to leave him there. They may find him come day—I don't care much—he gets fed twice a week.

Must go now,

Arrivederci,

Boxc.

OYSTER BAY GUARDIAN

for

OYSTER BAY'S NEWSPAPER
Since 1899

Phones: SYosset 6-1600 · 6-1601

SYOSSET MARKET
C. JANKE & SONS
CHOICE MEATS · FINE PROVISIONS · FROZEN FOODS
Opposite R. R. Station   Syosset, N. Y.

EAST NORWICH ESSO SERVICE
Robert Berran, Jr., Prop.
LUBRICATION · WASHING
TIRES · BATTERIES
ACCESSORIES
Corner Northern Boulevard and
Oyster Bay Road
East Norwich, L. I.
Tel. OYster Bay 6-0735

HOLIDAY BAKERS, Inc.
77 SOUTH STREET
OYSTER BAY, N. Y.

Main Bakery: Freeport
— Branches at —
Glen Cove · Manhasset · Hempstead

HAPPY BIRTHDAY

February:
20—Joseph Girolamo.
21—Reginald Butt, Peter Campanella.
23—Wesley Boone, Samuel Bozzello, Robert Murray.
24—Edward Arnold, Robert Denninger.
25—John Massa.
26—Isaac Tankard.
27—Joyce Reed, Beverly Tatro.
28—Leon Hirst, Carmine A. Bugliarelli, Raymond Anthony Kohn, Linda Monilawn, Savanah Reid.
29—Benjamin Fowler.

March:
2—Warrick Robinson.
3—Kenneth Willis, Virginia Woodward, Martha Evans.
6—Arthur De Madelar.
7—Serge Nepo.
9—Noah Walters, Virginia Furman.
11—Frederick Allen, Mary Anne Platt.
13—Robert Domiano, Roger Hunter.
14—Roy Smith, Mario Masmone, Derik Rosa.
15—Chester Martling.
17—Bill Andrews.
18—Shirley Hults, Kenneth Wright.

Can You Imagine?

1. Mary Ann Platt with her mind made up?
2. Edie, Marianne, and Willow not talking during shorthand class?
3. Nunzi P. coming to school on time?
4. The Varsity cheerleaders being appreciated by that certain few?
5. Seventh period study hall with a "full house?"
6. Dolores Szwejkowski screaming?
7. Miss Campanaro teaching Latin?
8. Tony Kohm not arguing?
9. Abe Bernstein?
10. Mr. Ruckel not smiling?
11. Mickey Minicozzi ever failing a subject?
12. Kathy Anos sitting still for five minutes?
13. Marcella without Ray?

Phone OYster Bay 6-2938

EMIL'S SERVICE STATION
SINCLAIR PRODUCTS
SERVICING AND REPAIRING
20 E. Main St., Oyster Bay, N. Y.

TEDDY'S
EXPERT TAILORING
CLEANING · PRESSING
We pick up and deliver
11 E. Main St.   Oyster Bay
OYster Bay 6-0833

Compliments of . . .

Roosevelt Candy Kitchen
52 Audrey Avenue   Oyster Bay, N. Y.
Phone OYster Bay 6-1769

Telephones: OYster Bay 6-9480 · 6-0481

HANOPHY'S MARKET

PRIME MEATS · POULTRY

PROVISIONS

101 SOUTH STREET   OYSTER BAY, L. I.

NORWICH MOTORS, Inc.

AT THE SIGN

Ford

EAST NORWICH

Route 25A · Opp. Rothmann's

Tel. OYster Bay 6-3232

Purple and Gold, 19 February 1953, 8.

"Voice of the Hamster"

Dear Sam,

Did it! Passed trig! I was taking it half-year, you know, with The Boys, and we finally succeeded in getting Faggiaducci to the point where he was completely fed up with us. He got so mad that the day of the Regents he refused to proctor the exam. So we were stuck with some neurotic Czech who screamed instead of talked.

Anyway, we started singing, "Do not forsake me, Faggiaducci," and he got purple and screamed—screamed, mind you, not yelled like Faggiaducci— "Shut up or I'll kick you all out!" Then he started swearing and insulting us and throwing things until finally he got us pretty riled. Now you know there's one thing meaner than The Boys, and that's The Boys riled. Sid Scully called the Czech something very uncomplimentary; Crazy Harrigan hit him from behind with a ruler; and Bob Woods tripped him with a chair when he swung at Sid. He headed out of the room, intending to call the principal. That did it! En masse, The Boys arose, surrounded the Czech, picked him up bodily, stuffed him in the dumbwaiter, and left him there until we could finish the exam in peace.

Faggiaducci had said that the best mark he had expected was somewhere in the low 60's; as it was, there was no mark lower than 92. (Don't ask me how we did it!) This, of course, had a severe psychological effect on Faggiaducci. He hasn't been to school in a week. I hear he had a breakdown. The Czech? Well, nobody uses that dumbwaiter shaft anymore, and so we decided to leave him there. They may find him some day—I don't care much—he gets fed twice a week.

> Must go now,
> Arrivederci,
> Bosc.

* * *

Purple and Gold, 19 March 1953, 2.

"Ye Legend of Sir Stupid and the Purple Knight"

"Ridiculous!" roared King Arthur, slamming his beer mug on the Round Table. "Purple, you say?"

"All purple, my liege," said Sir Launcelot, nervously wiping the foam from his face, "head to toes. Completely."

"I say! Most irregular. Well, what does he want?"

"He wants audience with you, my liege. It seems he's done ole

Cholmondesley in."

"Cholmondesley?"

"With an axe, your grace. A purple axe. He says he'll do the same to us all if we don't send a challenger to fight him in fair battle."

"Well?"

"Well, he—he's—twenty feet tall."

"Twenty! Oh, I say! Ghastly business! Who've we got crazy enough to fight him? How about you, Launcelot?"

"Oh, no, my liege. Cut my finger last night peeling potatoes. The pain is beastly."

"Rotten luck, old chap. Well," he addressed the knights of the round table, "there's a big purple idiot outside who's looking for a fight. Who's game?"

Then up spake Sir Bushwack, a sturdy youth with a broad beam and a low center of gravity: "Where is the bloke? I'm not afraid, even if he is twenty feet tall!" Sir Bushwack had been drinking.

Then spake King Arthur to Sir Launcelot, telling him to bid the knight enter. And Launcelot did this, and the horns sounded, and in staggered a tremendous giant, perhaps four feet in height, dragging behind him a ten-foot purple axe. He had a vast quantity of purple hair which fell down over his eyes, and was clad in purple armor, and his feet in purple sneakers. He led a noble steed, also purple, which resembled a cross between a Shetland pony and an armadillo.

King Arthur whispered to Launcelot, "I thought you said he was twenty feet tall."

"That's what he told me, your majesty."

"That's what he *what?* Why you . . ."

The rest of King Arthur's tirade was drowned out by the purple giant, who was bellowing in a mighty voice:

"Okay, I can beat any man in the house! I ain't scared of nobody 'cause you're all . . ." he hiccoughed ". . . chicken to fight me! Come on, who's first?"

Up spake Sir Bushwack, shouting, "I challenge thee, Sir Knight!"

The purple knight laughed. "Look what'sh challenging me! You slob, I can,—hic—can lick you with,—hic—one hand tied behind my back! Come ahead!" Then did the purple knight pick up the purple axe and begin to whirl it about his head, faster and faster. Sir Bushwack waddled up dubiously with sword in hand, feebly attempted to parry, then quickly retreated. The purple knight stood and laughed.

"Chicken, all of you! Scared to fight me! Har! Har!"

Suddenly, the horns sounded and into the hall rushed a very brave and manly knight, Sir Stupid.

"I say!" he shouted to all and sundry, "Old Fotheringay's run amok! He and his horse fell into that newly-pressed grape juice up at the distillery,

Purple and Gold

Published monthly by the students of
Oyster Bay High School

STAFF

Editor	Tony Kohn
Advertising Manager	Laura George
Advertising Assistants	June Hemrich, Emily Koehler
News Editors	Ruth McConie, Mary Alice Fedoroff, Betty Meehan
Exchange Editor	Mary Ann Platt
Copy Editors	Betty Ann Bruhns, Mary Thompson
Circulation Manager	Robert Weitzman
Circulation Assistants	Gary Flower, Martin Olsen
Make-Up Editors	Herman Bowman, Peggy Disbrow, Joan Alfano
Sports Editors	Charles Rothmann, Gladys Chisum
General Organization Editor	June Crawford
Humor Editor	John Nostrand
Head Typist	Willow Hunter

Proof Readers
Carla Hubbard, Althea Beglin

Special Writers
Denise Warren, Thomas Pynchon, Virginia Furman

Managing Editor	James George
Faculty Advisor	Mr. Kasius

March 19, 1953   Fifteen Cents

EDITORIAL

With one-half of the year gone, now might be the time for our G. O. to review the first semester's accomplishments. Amid the cheering that went on during the campaign last June, many promises were made by the candidates and the parties that supported them.

In view of the fact that one candidate from each party was elected, I suggested that a coalition of campaign promises take place. Some promises, made by more than one party, i.e., new uniforms for the J. V. Cheerleaders and more varied assemblies, have been carried out. However, some of the more progressive ideas that were expressed by individual parties have been pushed aside.

Dan Lambertson's party suggested that we have a faculty amateur hour. This was, and still is, a good suggestion. How about some action concerning it? Tom Griffin's and Angie Minicozzi's party proposed buying a victory flag. As of yet, there is no victory flag.

I realize that the parties that supported the various candidates no longer exist and, consequently, cannot lend their support to the ideas that their candidates suggested. Of course, it must be taken into consideration that action may even now be under way to fulfill the various promises, or that they may have been already considered and turned down. If this is not the case, however, I should like to state that, in my opinion, the officers, having been elected, have a certain obligation to the student body to fulfill the planks they ran on.

I would like, therefore, a statement from the officers concerning these and other ideas. I would like to find out how far we have come and how far we have to go. In short, I'd like to know what has happened to the progressive promises of last year's campaign. As the student body, we have the right to know!

Drops From The Faucet
By Two Drips

Has anybody seen a certain J. V. cheerleader making her bid for a senior from L. V.? And what about that popular girl with the initials A. M. Z. has her eye on a popular senior boy — N. G. has a senior interest too?

Someone told me that a junior girl managed to slip a declaration of love in poetry form into Bill's algebra book; I was also told that a very dear friend of hers has her eye on that tall, good-looking basketball star from Sea Cliff, R. J.. Could be! With the coming of spring, so many new romances seem to be in full bloom, especially among sophomores.

Who won all that poker money from Celeste's Saturday night, Madaline?

Do my eyes deceive me that a popular red-head is keeping company with "our star?" Another red-headed senior, who tells everyone to "keep punchin'," is complaining lately that "strange things" are happening.

Some boys have all the luck! What makes you so popular with the girls, Mr. Pilla? Lorraine, did I hear that you told a very cute serviceman in not uncertain terms? Shame on you! What senior keeps calling you up all the time, huh?

Quite a few similar "accidents" have been happening in the Gym lately. Some of them can be very embarrassing, can't they, Sally?

Ye Legend of Sir Stupid And the Purple Knight

"Ridiculous!" roared King Arthur, slamming his beer mug on the Round Table. "Purple, you say?"

"All purple, my liege," said Sir Launcelot, nervously wiping the foam from his face, "head to toes. Completely."

"I say! Most irregular. Well, what does he want?"

"He wants audience with you, my liege. It seems he's done old Cholmondesley in."

"Cholmondesley?"

"With an axe, your grace. A purple axe. He says he'll do the same to us all if we don't send a challenger to fight him in fair battle."

"Well?"

"Well, he — he's — twenty feet tall."

"Twenty! Oh, I say! Ghastly business! Who've we got crazy enough to fight him! How about you, Launcelot?"

"Oh, no, my liege. Cut my finger last night peeling potatoes. The pain is beastly."

"Rotten luck, old chap. Well," he addressed the knights of the round table, "there's a big purple idiot outside who's looking for a fight. Who's game?"

Then up spake Sir Bushwack, a sturdy youth with a broad beam and a low center of gravity. "Where is the bloke? I'm not afraid, even if he is twenty feet tall!" Sir Bushwack had been drinking.

Then spake King Arthur to Sir Launcelot, telling him to bid the knight enter. And Launcelot did this, and the horns sounded, and in staggered a tremendous giant, perhaps four feet in height, dragging behind him a ten-foot purple axe. He had a vast quantity of purple hair which fell down over his eyes, and was clad in purple armor, and his feet in purple sneakers. He led a noble steed, also purple, which resembled a cross between a Shetland pony and an armadillo.

King Arthur whispered to Launcelot, "I thought you said he was twenty feet tall."

"That's what he told me, your majesty."

"That's what he what? Why, you . . ."

The rest of King Arthur's tirade was drowned out by the purple giant, who was bellowing in a mighty voice:

"Okay, I can beat any man in the house! I ain't scared of nobody 'cause you're all . . ." he hiccoughed " . . . chicken to fight me! Come on, who's first?"

Up spake Sir Bushwack, shouting, "I challenge thee, Sir Knight!"

The purple knight laughed. "Look what'sh challenging me! You slob, I can, — hic — can lick you with, — hic — one hand tied behind my back! Come ahead!" Then did the purple knight pick up the purple axe and begin to whirl it about his head, faster and faster. Sir Bushwack waddled up dubiously with sword in hand, feebly attempted to parry, then quickly retreated. The purple knight stood and laughed.

"Chicken, all of you! Scared to fight me! Har! Har!"

Suddenly the horns sounded and into the hall rushed a very brave and manly knight, Sir Stupid.

"I say!" he shouted to all and sundry, "Old Fotheringay's run amok! He and his horse fell into that newly-pressed grape juice up at the distillery, and — . . ." Then he caught sight of the purple knight and stopped short. King Arthur started to laugh hysterically, spilling beer hither and yon.

"I say, old Fotheringay's gone and fallen into the wine vat! Old Fotheringay! Haw, Haw, Haw! Old Fotheringay's got high on grape juice! Haw! In the still of the knight?"

Old Fotheringay stood digesting this in silence. Then slowly he began to chuckle and whirl that axe.

"Oh, oh," Sir Stupid whispered to Arthur, "here he goes!" With a savage yell, Old Fotheringay charged the Round Table, swinging his axe. In an instant, the hall became the scene of a free-for-all. The purple knight was in the thick of the whole mess, smashing furniture, beer kegs, and anything else that happened to be in his way. The hall resounded with the clanging of swords, the splintering of wood, and the demoniacal chuckling of the purple knight. In the midst of the noise and confusion, Sir Stupid buttonholed Bushwack.

"Noble knight," he said, "art thou truly dedicated to thy liege?"

"Yes."

"And wouldst thou suffer discomfort to rid thy liege of this menace?"

"Surely," Sir Bushwack said absently, as he ducked a flying beer mug.

"That's all I wanted to know! Fotheringay! You feeble-minded halfwit cretin! Over here!"

Infuriated, the purple knight whirled toward Sir Stupid and arised his axe. Sir Stupid lifted the protesting Bushwack and hurled him bodily at Fotheringay. There was a loud, splintering smash as the purple knight went down, and then all was silent, except for the gurgling of beer from a shattered keg. Sir Stupid stood over the horizontal Fotheringay.

"Now, thou proud knight," roared Sir Stupid triumphantly, "now what hast thou to say?"

Slowly, the purple knight looked up and sneered "CHICKEN," he said.

Book Ends Meet

Last Thursday, March 26, 1953, the Library Assistants or "Book-ends," as we are known, discussed a very important point concerning you and the Library.

We have a system in the school whereby students may reserve books upon request. Also notices to the effect of books being overdue were given to home room teachers. This problem was discussed thoroughly because failure of some students to pick up reserves and to pay fines. We now have devised a system where the assistants deliver the notices. I am sure you could help them and others by picking up your reserve and returning the books and paying your fines as soon as you receive the notice.

If you have seen strange call letters on Catalog Cards like "FS," it means Film Strip. Each film strip in the Elementary and High School is now filed in the Catalog. They are for your convenience for Guidance or other purposes.

Book-end No. 8.

MEET THE FACULTY

I was a little skeptical about interviewing a teacher, particularly a new one, as I timidly entered room 105 to meet our new reading teacher, Mr. Berman. I introduced myself and asked him when it would be most convenient to interview him. "What about now?" he responded. (Why, I thought, this isn't going to be too bad! He seems to be a very cooperative man) — and cooperative he is, as I later found out.

After being graduated from Wagner College, Mr. Berman enrolled at N. Y. U. for graduate study. Before coming to O. B. H. S., he taught at the Washington Square Reading Center and at various public schools.

Originally from Staten Island, Mr. Berman has established his residence in Brooklyn with his wife, whom he met one summer when they were both counsellors at a camp. At this point he half-smiled and said, "Could you also mention the fact that I have to drive thirty miles to and from school every day?" Can you imagine anyone who has to drive sixty miles a day to and from work?

Although he was trained to be an aerial photographer in W.W.II, he never used this knowledge because other developments in his career overshadowed it.

Mr. Berman particularly likes good music and photography. He has a dog. Being from Brooklyn, he is naturally a Dodger fan. He has been working with children since the age of sixteen. It takes a lot of time and patience, but Mr. Berman enjoys it very much.

At this point time was running out, for the period was drawing to a close. I could have stayed and possibly found out much more about our new teacher, but I will leave that to you. I'm sure you'll like him, for he is very pleasing to talk to, has a friendly disposition, and can be easily recognized by his height and his broad shoulders.

165

and. . .". Then he caught sight of the purple knight and stopped short. King Arthur started to laugh hysterically, spilling beer hither and yon.

"I say, old Fotheringay's gone and fallen into the wine vat! Old Fotheringay! Haw, Haw, Haw! Old Fotheringay's got high on grape juice! Haw! In the still of the knight!"

Old Fotheringay stood digesting this in silence. Then slowly he began to chuckle and whirl that axe.

"Oh, oh," Sir Stupid whispered to Arthur, "here he goes!" With a savage yell, Old Fotheringay charged the Round Table, swinging his axe. In an instant, the hall became the scene of a free-for-all. The purple knight was in the thick of the whole mess, smashing furniture, beer kegs, and anything else that happened to be in his way. The hall resounded with the clanging of swords, the splintering of wood, and the demonaical chuckling of the purple knight. In the midst of the noise and confusion, Sir Stupid buttonholed Bushwack.

"Noble knight," he said, "art thou truly dedicated to thy leige?"

"Yes."

"And wouldst thou suffer discomfort to rid thy liege of this menace?"

"Surely," Sir Bushwack said absently, as he ducked a flying beer mug.

"That's all I wanted to know! Fotheringay! You feeble-minded halfwit cretin! Over here!"

Infuriated, the purple knight whirled toward Sir Stupid and raised his axe. Sir Stupid lifted the protesting Bushwack and hurled him bodily at Fotheringay. There was a loud, splintering smash as the purple knight went down, and then all was silent, except for the gurgling of beer from a shattered keg. Sir Stupid stood over the horizontal Fotheringay.

"Now, thou proud knight," roared Sir Stupid triumphantly, "now what hast thou to say?"

Slowly, the purple knight looked up and sneered. "CHICKEN," he said.

* * *

Purple and Gold, 19 March 1953, 8.

"The Boys"

In the past few weeks at O. B. H. S. there has arisen a newer, brighter star in the already brilliant constellation of our extracurricular activities. This organization evolved slowly and painfully; many factors contributed to its maturity (for lack of a better word). One has been the natural psychological manic phase prevalent in most seniors coupled with a compulsive-obsessive complex to apathy concerning schoolwork; in other words, goofing off and fooling around. Another has been a certain series of articles in the P. & G. which has fired the imagination of the group of students comprising this society.

"The Boys," for so this group is called, had heretofore been working in the shadow of anonymous immunity, and their names and faces were unknown save to their own compact enclave. But now the secret is out, for "The Boys" have finally reached a peak: they have gotten their pictures taken for the yearbook of '53.

This singular event took place at the beginning of sixth period on Thursday, February 26. This date is significant; it marks the beginning of a new era of student-teacher relations. Quietly, efficiently, a few couriers infiltrated the halls and classrooms. A whispered sentence, a tap on the shoulder, and another silently left class. Finally, the entire organization was assembled on the front steps of the school, the camera set up, the picture ready to be snapped. But wait! No Mr. X! (Mr. X, of course, being the math. teacher). Shouting enthusiastically, "The Boys" gathered under his class-room window, and began chanting, "We want X! We want X!"

Slowly, Mr. X approached the window, peered out through his horn-rimmed glasses and retreated hastily. The shouts grew louder; finally, timidly, Mr. X raised his hand, and said, "All right, all right. I'm coming." A roar went up, as "The Boys" cheered en masse, and finally Mr. X appeared, resplendent in bow tie and bop cardigan. The picture was snapped, and history was made.

From the Oyster Bay High School yearbook
   Oysterette (1953)

Best Student
Mary Thompson & Tom Pynchon

The Purple and Gold has carried on the old tradition of service to the school. It has also made its own new innovations. The principal one being a column by Tom Pynchon that has dealt with such learned subjects as the "Life and Times of Hamster High," a legend about a stupid knight, and, of course, the "Boys."

OYSTERETTE STAFF

This year our yearbook has been organized by a group of hard-working Sophs, Juniors and Seniors. Heading the art staff is William Goerl, with Judith Schwager as assistant editor; in the literary department, we have Thomas Pynchon as editor, and Herman Bowman as assistant editor; and on the business staff, Lucille Ianicello is business manager and Joan Alfano, assistant.

These staffs, composed of Sophomores, Juniors, and Seniors, worked seventh periods and after school, blocking out dummies, writing articles, determining which photos go where, how many words on this page, what size type in that heading; all the myriad little problems and responsibilities that attend the publication of a yearbook.

A big vote of thanks goes to Mr. DiLillo, our photographer, and to the members of the staffs themselves, whose untiring work really is the essence of our '53 Oysterette. Our biggest debt, however, and our greatest thanks are owed to our faculty adviser, Mrs. Viatori.

So, another year has rolled around, and the '53 Oysterette staff mops its brow, and thankfully leaves all its "little problems" to future Oysterette staffs with best wishes for success.

171

Cast of senior class play, Kaufman and Hart's *You Can't Take It with You.*
Pynchon (below) was student director.

SENIOR CLASS WILL

JIM GEORGE leaves his executive ability to Bernard Murphy.

CHARLIE ROTHMANN leaves his suave manners and debonnaire character to Dennis Dodd.

BOB GUNTER leaves his car to the tow-truck.

GIL HERBERT leaves his curiosity to Mr. Sparrow.

DOLORES SZWEJKOWSKI leaves her gorgeous wardrobe to the Junior Girls.

MARY ANN PLATT leaves her many admirers——

BOBBY DARHINGER leaves his moose horn to Roberta Wind.

GLADYS HORNOSKY leaves her cheering uniform to any good seamstress who wants it.

RUTH McCONIE leaves her "flirty eyes" to Wilma Pinkerton.

MARTIN OLSEN shall return!

JOHN NOSTRAND leaves his presidency to anyone who wishes it.

TEDDY HICKS leaves his bow ties to Mr. Porcino.

HANK BOWMAN leaves his jokes to any fool who'll listen.

DENNIE WARREN leaves her high heels and earrings to Miss Mulder.

DAN SMOLNIK leaves his concession rights to Ship's Point to Emilio Donisi.

RICHARD ZANTS leaves his chem book to Kathi Kavanagh.

PEGGY DISBROW leaves her raised eyebrow to Sally Withers.

LAURA GEORGE leaves her sweaters to Sandy Still.

BETTY MEEHAN leaves her ultra-sophistication to Gloria Marotti.

The Knight brothers just leave**

JUNE CRAWFORD and SAM BOZZELLO leave their squabbles to Jean Dietrich and Mike Fessel.

CARLA HUBBARD leaves her curly locks to Beatrice Tharp.

JUDY MILLS leaves her place at Jackson's Playhouse to Marion Weatherby.

EDITH KRAFT leaves her summer bungalow in Centre Island to anyone who's fool enough to take it.

MARY ALICE FEDEROFF leaves her sweet ways to Joyce Fielstead.

NORMA SPRAGUE leaves her lovely voice to John Stetson.

GARY FLOWER leaves his long wavy locks to Rick Robinson.

PETIE BEGLIN leaves her ability on the organ to Ann Labounsky.

BETTY ANN BRUHNS leaves her calm disposition to Jane Crawley.

TOMMY PYNCHON leaves his big vocabulary to Jimmy Donovan.

GINNY FURMAN leaves her membership in the "Bachelor Girls Club" to Dotti Platt.

RHODA CRAWFORD leaves her cigarette case to Willy Jane Zandbergen.

MacNAMARA leaves his high opinion of himself to Tennessee.

JUNE HEMRICH leaves her cheeriness to Dotty Jones.

JOAN PARENTE leaves her 3rd period lunches to Barbara Stanley.

BOB FORREST leaves his poetic ability to Ken Clark.

TONY KOHM & LUCILLE IANNICELLO leave their arguments to Mr. Gaynor.

DOLORES HAUSER leaves her questions to Mickey Minicozzi.

PAT PARSHLEY leaves her grin to Palma Iasiello.

JOAN ALFANO leaves her knowledge of French to Sandy Kressly.

MIKE BAITZ leaves Irene under the watchful eye of Mr. Halladay.

JOE GALASSO leaves his well-dressed appearance to Larry Remsen.

The girls in Law class leave Mr. Carr reluctantly.

JUDY SCHWAGER leaves her giddiness to Abe Bernstein.

DAN LAMBERTSON leaves his "line" to Serge Nepo.

BOB WEITZMAN leaves his "humor" to David Baur.

BILL GOERL & EDITH leave their space in the hall to John Covino & Dolly.

EMILY KOEHLER leaves the sailors in Washington to the Junior Class.

ARLENE MARTLING leaves her knowledge of bookkeeping to Angie Minicozzi.

ALYCE MARTIN leaves her eyelashes to Barbara Schuller.

The rest of the class just leaves.

**(They Hope!)

MATH CLUB

The Math Club is one of our newest organizations at Oyster Bay, and under the guidance of our faculty adviser, Mr. Porcino, we constitute also one of the most informal groups. Mr. Porcino, better known as a math teacher, dance instructor, and linguist, gets as big a kick out of the organization as its members do.

At the time this article was written officers had yet to be chosen and a constitution drawn up, but we were already planning our first activity: a play, to be written and acted by members of the Club.

We also plan to continue this organization on into next year and the years following, and each year to have an induction of Juniors who plan to take trig and solid. In this way we will perpetuate the immortal name of the "the Boys," and the spirit of good-natured fun attending thereto.

Pynchon and a few of "The Boys"

NATIONAL HONOR SOCIETY

EL CIRCULO ESPANOL

The Spanish Club elected Annette Raymon as president, Charlie Rothmann as vice-president and Betty Meehan as secretary. Alan Bishop was elected as the Spanish I representative.

The club meetings consisted of humorous skits, songs, talks, refreshments and something new in the way of quizzes. Both the Spanish II and III classes sprang surprise quizzes. The club also had successful Christmas and Valentine parties.

Muchas gracias to Senorita Campanaro for helping to make this a most enjoyable year for her grateful amigos.

PYNCHON, THOMAS

"Pynch"; P & G; Yearbook; Trade Fair 2,
3, 4; Sr. Play student director; Spanish
Club 3, 4; Honor Society 3, 4; likes pizza;
dislikes hypocrites; pet possession, a type-
writer; aspires to be a physicist.